A Roadkill Opera

Piano/Vocal

STEPHAN ALEXANDER PARKER

Music by Ferdinando Paer

Piano reduction arrangement
by Brian Clark, Prima la musica!

Poster on cover courtesy of Hatch Show Print

Cover photograph courtesy of DJ Choupin

Roadkill logo courtesy of Eric Scholl

ISBN-13: 978-1481921688
ISBN-10: 1481921681

for Elaine & Frank

CONTENTS

	Workshop Concert Program & Merchandise	i
1	Overture	1
2	Impress Them	8
3	In A Clearing	16
4	Cod Piece Dining	26
5	Jello	37
6	Different Things	38
7	Geo	44
8	Suppose	57
9	Butterflies	61
10	Torn Down	70
11	Opening Night	82
12	Finished	97
13	Glory	107

PLAY BALL!

THE (UNOFFICIAL) LAST TWO WORDS OF THE U.S. NATIONAL ANTHEM

OPERA MEETS COMEDY IN ARTOMATIC 2012 SHOWCASE OF "OPENING NIGHT: A ROADKILL OPERA"

Jeffrey Dokken, Music Director and Conductor for the Symphony Orchestra of Arlington, to Lead Five Opera Singers and an Eight-Person Chamber Orchestra in "Opening Night: A Roadkill Opera"

CRYSTAL CITY, VA (June 4, 2012) — This week marks the debut of "Opening Night: A Roadkill Opera," a new opera workshop, at Artomatic 2012, the Washington area's largest free creative arts event. Set to classical music from 1804 and crossed with a backstage comedy set in 1988, the 59-minute opera tells the story of the hour before the lights go up on opening night for a comedy improv troupe in Jackson Hole, Wyoming. Workshops or open rehearsals and the June 9th concert performance are free and open to the public on the stages of Artomatic at 1851 South Bell Street in Crystal City, Va.

"We're pleased to bring this innovative and amusing opera workshop to Artomatic this year," said Barry Schmetter, Artomatic events director. "The piece was conceived at Artomatic some years ago and is being directed and performed by some extremely talented individuals."

"Opening Night: A Roadkill Opera" is being workshopped by Jeffrey Dokken, Music Director and Conductor for the Symphony Orchestra of Arlington. "This project has become extremely dear to my heart and I am working hard to ensure its immediate and long term success," said Dokken.

Maestro Dokken became involved with the project after long-time Artomatic exhibitor Stephan Alexander Parker completed this new English libretto, begun and roughed-out during Artomatic 2004. A search for interested producing partners was launched at Artomatic 2009, and ended in 2012 when Dokken received a copy of the score through a mutual friend, Martine Micozzi, who performs on flute in this concert.

Music from 1804. Action set in 1988. A new opera (in just 59 minutes)

"Opening Night: A Roadkill Opera" tells the story of the hour before the lights go up on opening night for a comedy improv troupe in Jackson Hole, Wyoming—the Roadkill On A Stick Frozen Foods Theatre Company. Based (loosely) on a true story from a fast-developing tourist town, this original English libretto by Parker is set to music by Ferdinando Paer (Napoleon's maître de chapelle).

It took 25 years to identify the classical opera Parker recorded off an FM station, and another 5 years to acquire the score.

The new opera is being workshopped at Artomatic for the first time ever. For that reason, performers will not be costumed, nor will there be sets, props, or blocking. The cast includes Laura Wehrmeyer (Holly), soprano; Andrew Webster (Eddie), baritone; David Timpane (Stephan), bass; Krista Monique McClellan (Debby), soprano; and John Dellaporta (Dave), tenor.

A display on the first floor of Artomatic provides the backstory to the opera, and an opportunity to view the score.

The performance is one of many featured at the month-long arts event. Artomatic 2012 is the largest ever event, featuring work and performances by more than 1300 artists, performers, musicians, filmmakers, fashion designers, and creatives of all kinds in a 380,000 square-foot office building in Crystal City, Va. The event runs through June 23.

Can you spot the X things wrong on the cover? Email your discoveries to roadkillopera@icloud.com

Laura Wehrmeyer (Holly) has appeared locally as Josephine in *HMS Pinafore* with The Washington Savoyards; Mabel in *Pirates of Penzance* with The Arlington Players; and Desirée in *Desirée*, Arsena in *The Gypsy Baron*, and Rose in *Ruddigore* with Victorian Lyric Opera Company. She appeared in the Symphony Orchestra of Arlington's inaugural concert last season, and again as a soloist in the SOA Goes Broadway concert this past January. Laura performs regularly with the In Series, and has appeared as Gianetta in *Love Potion #1*, Niña Tula in *Maria La O,* Natasha in *From Shuffle to Showboat,* Doxie in *Casino Paradise,* Susanna/Bastienne/Blondchen in *WAM!* (with the Washington Ballet), Frasquita/ensemble in *Carmen*, and Norah in *Noël and Cole*. Musical theatre credits include Johanna in *Sweeney Todd*, Lily in *The Secret Garden*, Christine in Toby's *Phantom of the Opera*, and swing/ensemble in Signature Theatre's *Les Misérables*. Laura is the soprano section leader and soloist at St. John's Norwood Parish Episcopal Church in Bethesda, where she recently sang the role of the Evangelist in the Heinrich Schütz St. John Passion.

Andrew Webster (Eddie), baritone, is an undergraduate student at James Madison University where he is currently pursuing degrees in both Vocal Performance and Business. He has appeared in a number of productions, including the roles of Peter in Humperdinck's *Hänsel und Gretel*, Aeneas in Purcell's *Dido and Aeneas*, and Captain Von Trapp in *The Sound of Music.* Andrew is currently in the studio of Professor David Newman.

George Spelvin (Marvin) has an extensive biography on Wikipedia, the free encyclopedia.

David Timpane (Stephan), a native of Arlington, VA area, earned a Master of Music degree in Vocal Performance from Manhattan School of Music in 1994. Since graduating, he has performed both nationally and internationally as a soloist in operas and oratorios. He has been featured regularly in performances of Handel's *Messiah*, Brahms' *Requiem*, Fauré's *Requiem* and numerous other oratorios. His operatic repertoire includes Marcello and Schaunard in *La Bohème*, Silvio in *I Pagliacci*, Gianni Schicci in *Gianni Schicci,* Falke in *Die Fledermaus* and Oreste in *Iphigènie en Tauride*. David was named "a voice to listen for" by Opera News.

Krista Monique McClellan (Debby) is a Brazilian-American lyric soprano from Washington, DC. She has performed leading roles including Dido (Dido & Aeneas); Donna Anna (Don Giovanni); Lucy (The Telephone) and Giulietta (Les Contes d'Hoffmann). Recently, she performed at the Embassy of Germany in Washington, DC as part of the Emerging Singers Program of the Wagner Society of Washington. She is a frequent recitalist and has performed numerous concerts throughout the United States and Brazil.

John Dellaporta (Dave). Born and raised in Ft. Lauderdale, FL, John relocated to the Washington, DC area to study at the Catholic University of America's Benjamin T. Rome School of Music. After completing the school's prestigious musical theatre program, he remained in the area, working with Olney Theatre Center, Adventure Theatre, Bay Theatre Company, Toby's Dinner Theatre, the Washington Savoyards, Limelight Theatre, Open Circle Theatre, and, most recently, the New Musicals Foundation's *Who's Your Baghdaddy? Or, How I Started the Iraq War*, which was voted as "Pick of Fringe - Best Overall Show" and enjoyed an extended hit run. Other favorite roles: Matt in *The Fantasticks*, Strephon in *Iolanthe*, Man 1 in *Closer than Ever*, and appearing as a company member in Helen Hayes-honored productions of *Annie* and *Titanic: the Musical.*

Jeffrey Sean Dokken (Music Director and Conductor). Maestro Dokken is one of today's most exciting and vibrant conductors, composers, and musicians. Over the past decade Jeff has performed all across the United States, and in some of America's greatest venues including the Kennedy Center and Carnegie Hall. In December, Dokken had the distinct pleasure of conducting at the White House in Washington, DC. In May 2012, Jeff had the incredible opportunity to conduct tenor Jackson Caesar in concert with one of the world's leading gospel choirs, Patrick Lundy and the Ministers of Music. During 2012, Jeff will be conducting across the United States and in South America with the Symphony Orchestra of Arlington and as a guest conductor of many leading orchestras, soloists, and choirs. In addition to composing, conducting, and performing on opera, classical and musical theatre CDs and DVDs, Jeff is the musical consultant for the largest health care corporation in America, Kaiser Permanente. Dokken maintains a private voice and piano studio and is active as an educator and adjudicator.

Opening Night

A Roadkill Opera

roadkillopera.com

Workshop rehearsals & concert performance of a new opera, June 2012

Music from 1804 by Ferdinando Paer
Libretto by Stephan Alexander Parker

Jeffrey Dokken, Music Director & Conductor

Program

1. Overture..................Orchestra
2. Impress Them.........Holly
3. In A Clearing...........Eddie & Holly
4. Cod Piece Dining...Stephan, Holly, Eddie
5. Jello.........................Holly, Stephan & Eddie
6. Different Things.......Debby
7. Geo..........................Dave, Debby & Stephan
8. Suppose..................Debby
9. Butterflies................Holly
10. Torn Down.............Stephan & Debby
11. Opening Night........Stephan, Dave, Debby
12. Finished..................Holly, Dave, Stephan, Debby & Eddie
13. Glory........................Dave, Eddie, Holly, Debby & Stephan

Cast

HOLLY, radio newscaster / lead actress......................Soprano........... **Laura Wehmeyer**
EDDIE, whitewater raft guide / lead actor..................Baritone.......... **Andrew Webster**
MARVIN, mechanic /set builder, stage manager......Banging Nails...**George Spelvin**
STEPHAN, rival raft guide / director...........................Bass.............. **David Timpane**
DEBBY, waitress / box office manager.......................Soprano.... **Krista Monique McClellan**
DAVE, has a real job / accompanist..............................Tenor.............. **John Dellaporta**

Orchestra

Flute......... **Martine Micozzi**
Clarinet...... **Jeannine Altavilla**
Bassoon...... **Sarah Robinson**
Trumpet..... **Michael Thompson**
Violin I....... **Frank Peracchia**
Violin II...... **Holly Petty**
Violin III...... **Kendall Isadore**
Cello............ **Kathy Augustine**

Roadkill logo by Eric Scholl

Production Notes

This story is told through the sung lyrics; certain plot points can be made clearer through supertitles and stage direction (if the action is mounted). For concert performances, if the director prefers, brief monologues are provided between songs. The monologues can also be used if supertitles are not feasible. Stage directions and optional monologues are provided below. The monologues are to be spoken before the music for the song.

1. **Overture** (Eddie): Cue slideshow to start with the music.

    Hi. My name is Ed. The story you are about to, let's say, "enjoy," is true. Only the names have been changed to protect the naive.

    What's that? Really? Oh. Okay, I'll do it over right this time.

    Huh. Writers.

    Hi. My name is Ed. The story you are about to see is true-ish. The names have not been changed.

    Are you sure this is a good idea?
    All right.

    Well. So. This stuff really happened, sort of, mostly, on July 4th weekend in 1988. Think "Yellowstone fires."

    We were the best sketch comedy improv group in Jackson Hole. We were the only sketch comedy improv group in Jackson Hole. I don't think there were any other sketch comedy improv groups in Wyoming at the time.

    Oh, that's right, time. "Time flies like an arrow. Fruit flies like a banana." Groucho Marx. But I digress...

    Time. It is one hour before we start our first public performance. It is Opening Night. While you are listening to the overture, here are some pictures of Wyoming from 1948 and more recently. If you like them, prints are available at a very reasonable price.

    What? No, I am not being too commercial. If I was being commercial, I would have told them that we have posters, hats, and bottle openers for sale. That would be commercial.

    Don't you talk to me like that, I'm your partner in this so-called business.

You know, they call show business "show business," because it is also about business--otherwise they'd call it "show show." Yep. But you notice nobody ever calls opera "opera business?"

But you can change that. Yessirree. Buy lots of stuff at intermission. That'll show 'em. When the going gets tough, the tough go shopping....for opera souvenirs.

And when you leave the theatre, remember this important message:

If you see roadkill, think opera.
roadkillopera.com.

My name is Ed.

(Bows).

2. **Impress Them** (Holly):

   Hi! My name is Holly. I do the radio news at KMTN, the Mountain. I really want to be a disc jockey. I can impress my bosses with this show.

3. **In A Clearing** (Eddie):

   Hi! My name is Ed. Animals are funny. If we add more animals to the show, it will be funnier. Then we can sell more tickets. Right, Marv?

   (Marv shakes his head and walks off-stage).

   My name is Ed.

   (Bows. During the song, Eddie can display items he is suggesting, such as a big brochure advertising Louie's Llamas. If he has a cutout of a llama's head on a stick, he can grab a camera from Holly and hang it on the llama's neck).

4. **Cod Piece Dining** (Stephan):

   Hi! My name is Stephan. I think I've nailed down the running order of the sketches, the set list. I'll just go over it with Eddie and Holly. I wonder if I've had too much coffee?

   (As he enters the scene, Stephan carries in one hand a large posterboard with the running order written on it, and in the other hand a large plastic coffee mug labeled "Vuarnet Café").

5. **Jello** (Stephan):

   What was that, Marv? "Churning Jello" will spill Jello and stain the floor? We can't afford to lose our deposit on this showroom. We'll have to cut "Churning Jello" from the show.

   (Stephan uses a marker to cross out "Churning Jello" on the poserboard. Marv can start to move a large butter churn with a Jello label on it to the wings as Holly and Eddie enter).

6. **Different Things** (Debby): *is alone on stage, musing on the fate of the troupe if the show is not a hit.*

   Hi! My name is Debby. I'm not in the show, I'm just working the box office.

   (Debbie shows the cashbox and tickets).

7. **Geo** (Dave): *enters and tells her how great it is to be in showbiz. Debby and Stephan debate the pros and cons of various Geo models as they advise Dave on what kind of car to buy for his grandfather.*

   Hi! My name is Dave. I'm doing the music for the show. This gig will help me buy a new car. There are great financing deals through Geo, this new small-car line at the Chevy dealer. I just need to decide on which model.

   (Dave holds a big brochure with the Geo models in it, which Debby and Stephan point to when making their points: Metro, Tracker, Prizm, and Storm).

8. **Suppose** (no dialogue): *Debby wonders what will happen if the show is successful.*

9. **Butterflies** (Holly): *gets butterflies as the curtain approaches.*

   Oh, no, I am getting stage fright.

10. **Torn Down** (no dialogue): *Stephan informs Debby that the showroom is being torn down. They reminisce on the great acts that have played the room. Marv watches.*

11. **Opening Night** (Stephan): *Stephan gives Dave a pep talk.*

    Our show really depends on Dave's music. I'll just give him a pep talk. Unfortunately, I think we both have a crush on Debby

12. **Finished** (no dialogue). *Marv whispers in Holly's ear. Holly enters, upset at the news that the room is being torn down. Eddie enters and suggests ways to annoy the town.*

13. **Glory** (Marv): *Marv bangs the gong three times; he might carry a sign and/or call out:*

    House is open!

The Roadkill Opera Merchandise

The items below can be ordered at roadkillopera@icloud.com or 240-277-6640.

The commemorative Hatch Show Print letterpress poster from the workshop concert performance on June 9, 2012. Only 120 posters were printed to commemorate the first public opportunity to hear Opening Night: A Roadkill Opera. All 120 posters were brought to the workshop concert performance. These 14 inch x 22 inch red and black ink letterpress posters were produced by Hatch Show Print, one of the oldest working letterpress print shops in America. Turn-of-the-century Hatch posters were used to promote vaudeville, circus, and minstrel shows across the country. There's a reason why music lovers, Americana buffs, graphic arts collectors and designers, and commercial advertisers of all persuasions continue to turn to Hatch for inspiration.

Poster only, 14 inches x 22 inches: $15   Framed, 17 inches x 25 inches: $30

The paperback book of one act plays and short stories. In one place for the first time, you can get the collection of Stephan Alexander Parker's one acts and shorts, including the libretto for Opening Night: A Roadkill Opera. *If You See Roadkill, Think Opera* includes stories inspired by living in Jackson Hole, Wyoming; Nashville, Tennessee; Orlando, Florida; Branson, Missouri; and Chicago, Illinois.

The paperback book: *If You See Roadkill, Think Opera*
6 x 9 in., 156 pages: $12.99 ISBN-13: 978-1481924047
ISBN: 1481924044 Digital versions also available

The Opening Night bottle opener, bumper sticker, and apron, with the original logo for Roadkill On A Stick Frozen Foods Theatre Company. This bottle opener, bumper sticker, and apron sport the original logo designed by Eric Scholl for the original production of the improvisational sketch comedy review *Roadkill Live!!!* that opened on Independence Day weekend 1988 in Jackson, Wyoming. Eric's logo has also been incorporated into the Hatch commemorative poster. Black letters on stainless steel (bottle opener). Black letters on white vinyl (bumper sticker). Blue letters embroidered on three-pocket Lands End khaki (apron).

Bottle opener, 1.5 x 7 in.: $8 Bumper sticker, 3 x 6 in.: $2 Apron (not shown): $18

The hat with the logo for A Roadkill Opera. The logo on this hat was adapted by the talented staff at Lands End, which also produced these hats in 100 percent cotton. The black hats were produced for the stage crew, the white hats for the public.

Black hat: $12 White hat: $10

The black bumper sticker with the tag line. The story of how A Roadkill Opera came to be is long and involved, as related in the short story by Stephan Alexander Parker. Taken as a whole though, the moral of the story is "If you see roadkill, think opera." White letters on black vinyl.

Black bumper sticker, 3 x 10 in.: $3

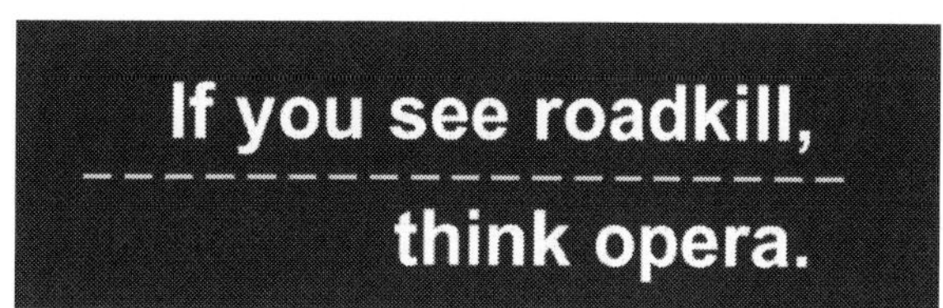

You Can Play & Sing Every Note With the Score & Parts

A Roadkill Opera: Piano/Vocal
Every note for the singers and piano accompaniment—perfect for rehearsals or for following along with the show.

142 pages, 8.5 x 11 inches, ISBN-13: 978-1481921688, ISBN-10: 1481921681: $18

A Roadkill Opera: Orchestral Score & Libretto
Follow along with the full orchestral score and libretto. Parts sold separately (see below). Please note that rights to perform *A Roadkill Opera* in public must also be secured separately.

250 pages, 8.5 x 11 inches, ISBN-13: 978-1482607987, ISBN-10: 1482607980: $18

A Roadkill Opera: Parts for Wind Instruments
Every note for flutes, oboes, clarinets, bassoons, horns, and trumpets.

168 pages, 8.5 x 11 inches, ISBN-13: 978-1482597752, ISBN-10: 1482597756: $18

A Roadkill Opera: Parts for Timpani & String Instruments
Every note for timpani, violin 1, violin 2, viola, viola transposed for violin 3, bass, violincello. Please note that all bass notes are within the playing range of cello.

222 pages, 8.5 x 11 inches, ISBN-13: 978-1482597790, ISBN-10: 1482597799: $18

A Roadkill Opera: Large Print Libretto & Parts for Vocals Lyrics in large print plus every note for Holly, Eddie, Stephan, Debby, and Dave.

154 pages, 8.5 x 11 inches, ISBN-13: 978-1482634563, ISBN-10: 1482634562: $18

The recordings. If you plan to perform numbers from the show for friends, in class, or in public, practice along to the original workshop cast recording, or take it one step further and play along with a recording that has your part left open for you to perform. CDs, $18 each. Downloadable tracks available, too.

A Roadkill Opera (Original Workshop Cast)

A Roadkill Opera, Wanted: Flutes & Oboes
A Roadkill Opera, Wanted: Horns & Trumpets
A Roadkill Opera, Wanted: Timpani
A Roadkill Opera, Wanted: Violin 2
A Roadkill Opera, Wanted: Bass
A Roadkill Opera, Wanted: Holly
A Roadkill Opera, Wanted: Stephan
A Roadkill Opera, Wanted: Dave
A Roadkill Opera, Wanted: Wind Instruments
A Roadkill Opera, Wanted: Clarinets
A Roadkill Opera, Wanted: Bassoons
A Roadkill Opera, Wanted: Violin 1
A Roadkill Opera, Wanted: Viola/Violin 3
A Roadkill Opera, Wanted: Violincello
A Roadkill Opera, Wanted: Eddie
A Roadkill Opera, Wanted: Debby
A Roadkill Opera, Wanted: String Instruments
A Roadkill Opera, Wanted: Vocals

Contact the publisher and author at roadkillopera@icloud.com or 240-277-6640.

The Story

The action takes place on Independence Day weekend 1988 in Jackson, Wyoming. Holly is alone onstage, giving herself a pep talk an hour before the house opens on opening night for *Roadkill Live!!!*, the first show by a local sketch comedy troupe—Roadkill On A Stick Frozen Foods Theatre Company. Eddie enters, in high spirits, intent on selling out the house. Marvin hammers together the scenery. An over-caffeinated Stephan enters, and goes over the running order of the sketches with Eddie and Holly. "My Breakfast with Booboo" makes it into the show. "Churning Jello" is cut.

Debby is alone on stage, musing on the fate of the troupe if the show is not a hit. Dave enters and tells her how great it is to be in showbiz. Debby and Stephan debate the pros and cons of various Geo models as they advise Dave on what kind of car to buy for his grandfather. Alone again, Debby wonders what will happen to the troupe if the show is successful. Holly gets butterflies as the curtain approaches.

Stephan informs Debby that the showroom is being torn down. They reminisce on the great acts that have played the room.

Stephan gives Dave a pep talk, and they both flirt with Debby. Holly enters, upset at the news that the room is being torn down. Eddie enters and suggests ways to annoy the town. Marv rings a bell three times and announces that the house is open. The cast greets the audience and invites them to enjoy the show, highlighting the sketches to come.

Opening Night

A stage in a bar showroom in Jackson Hole. At the back on each side is a dressing area also used for prop storage. In front on the right is the accompanist's area. It is Independence Day weekend 1988, an hour before the house opens for Roadkill Live!!!, *the first show by the Roadkill On A Stick Frozen Foods Theatre Company. Music plays as the lights go up.*

Instrumentation

Individual parts are gathered in 3 publications for (a) wind instruments, (b) timpani & string instruments, and (c) vocals. You can play along to *A Roadkill Opera (Original Workshop Cast)* or, if you prefer, play with the recording (minus your part) in the *Roadkill Opera, Wanted* series.

PART #	Parts included	1 Overture	2 Impress Them	3 In A Clearing	4 Cod Piece Dining	5 Jello	6 Different Things	7 Geo	8 Suppose	9 Butterflies	10 Torn Down	11 Opening Night	12 Finished	13 Glory	TOTAL NUMBERS (OF 13)
	Wind Instruments														
1	Flutes 1, 2	1	1	1	1	1	1		1	1		1	1	1	11
2	Oboes 1, 2	1	1	1	1	1	1	1	1	1	1	1	1	1	13
3	Clarinets in C 1, 2	1											1	1	3
	Clarinets in B-flat 1, 2		1					1	1		1	1			5
	Clarinets in A 1, 2			1								1		1	3
4	Bassoons 1, 2	1	1	1	1	1	1	1	1	1	1	1	1	1	13
5	Horns in C 1, 2	1			1				1						3
	Horns in E-flat 1, 2		1					1	1		1	1		1	6
	Horns in A 1, 2			1		1	1								3
	Horns in G 1, 2									1			1		2
	Horns in D 1, 2											1		1	2
6	Trumpets in C 1, 2	1													1
	Trumpet in B-flat							1							1
	Trumpets in D 1, 2											1		1	2
	Timpani & String Instruments														
7	Timpani	1						1				1		1	4
8	Violin 1	1	1	1	1	1	1	1	1	1	1	1	1	1	13
9	Violin 2	1	1	1	1	1	1	1	1	1	1	1	1	1	13
10	Viola / Violin 3	1	1	1	1	1	1	1	1	1	1	1	1	1	13
11	Bassi	1	1	1	1	1	1	1	1	1	1	1	1	1	13
	Violincello					1	1								2
	Vocals														
12	HOLLY (Soprano)		1	1	1	1				1			1	1	7
13	EDDIE (Baritone)			1	1	1							1	1	5
14	STEPHAN (Bass)				1	1		1			1	1	1	1	7
15	DEBBY (Soprano)						1	1	1		1	1	1	1	7
16	DAVE (Tenor)							1				1	1	1	4
	PARTS IN NUMBER	11	10	11	11	12	10	13	11	9	10	16	14	18	

Recordings available:

A Roadkill Opera (Original Workshop Cast)

A Roadkill Opera, Wanted: Flutes & Oboes
A Roadkill Opera, Wanted: Horns & Trumpets
A Roadkill Opera, Wanted: Timpani
A Roadkill Opera, Wanted: Violin 2
A Roadkill Opera, Wanted: Bass
A Roadkill Opera, Wanted: Holly
A Roadkill Opera, Wanted: Stephan
A Roadkill Opera, Wanted: Dave
A Roadkill Opera, Wanted: Wind Instruments
A Roadkill Opera, Wanted: Clarinets
A Roadkill Opera, Wanted: Bassoons
A Roadkill Opera, Wanted: Violin 1
A Roadkill Opera, Wanted: Viola/Violin 3
A Roadkill Opera, Wanted: Violincello
A Roadkill Opera, Wanted: Eddie
A Roadkill Opera, Wanted: Debby
A Roadkill Opera, Wanted: String Instruments
A Roadkill Opera, Wanted: Vocals

Contact the publisher and author at roadkillopera@icloud.com or 240-277-6640.

1. Overture

24 Allegro con spirito
p
fz
fz
29
fz
fz
p
fz
p
fz
p
fz
34
p
fz
ff
39
fz
fz
43
fz
fz
46
49

52
55
fz
fz
60
dolce
p
65
70
dolce
75
81
p

85
f
ff
pp
90
f
p
f
p
96
Andante di prima
100
104
ff
108
112
117

121
f
124
127
6
6
6
fz
fz
fz
131
6
fz
p
cresc.
ff
dolce
137
p
142
147
152

157
161
164
167
fz
fz
172
fz
fz
177
fz
fz
fz
fz
fz
fz
181
fp
fz
fp
fz
fp

184
fp
188
191
fz
6
fz
6
6
6
3
fz
196
3
fz
3
fz
201 Andante come sopra
dolce
205
209
p
f

2. Impress Them

21
H.
[sim.]
p

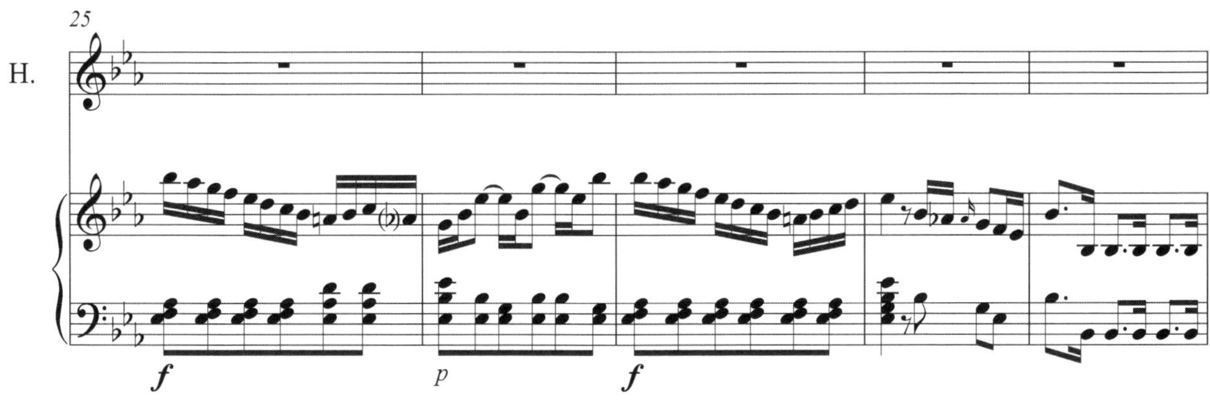
25
H.
f
p
f

30
H.
To -night my-y goal is to go out and im - press them all for once!
p
f

36
H.
Im - press them, im - press them, to - night!
p
f

41
H.
Im-press them. Im-
p
f
p
f
p
f

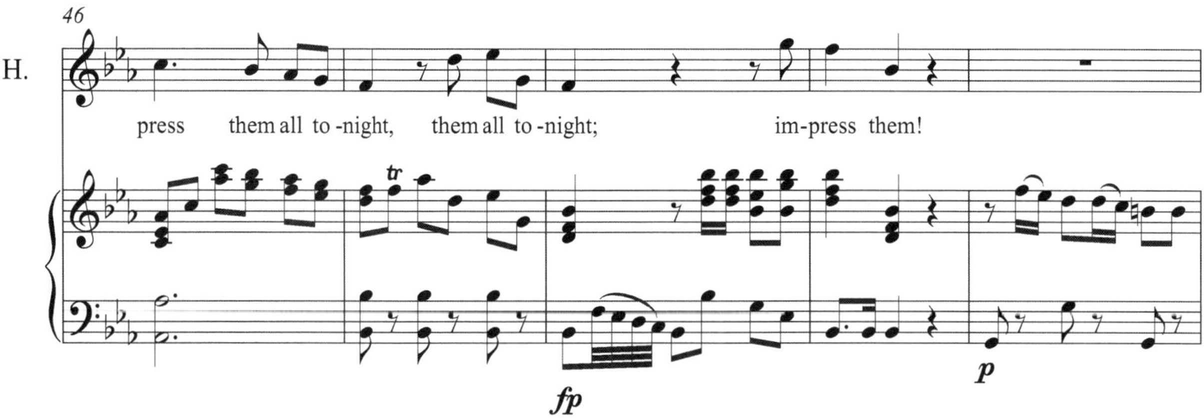
46
H.
press them all to -night, them all to -night; im-press them!
tr
fp
p

51
H.
I must get them to pro-mote me. I
fp

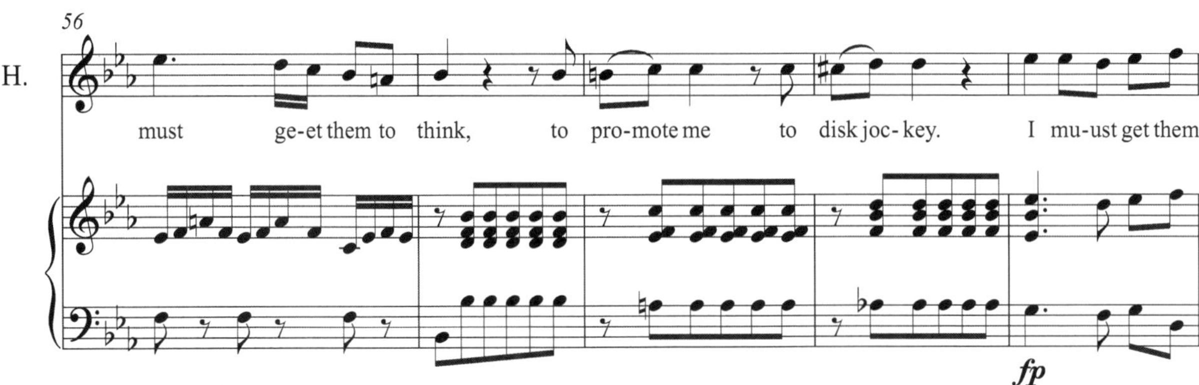
56
H.
must ge-et them to think, to pro-mote me to disk joc- key. I mu-ust get them
fp

colla parte
a piacere
61
H.
to pro - mote me, to be on air, to be a real disk joc-
rinf
fp

66
Andantino
H.
key. My dear, this may be my last chance to move from news to dee - jay. My
pizz.
pizz.

71
H.
dear, this may be my chance to move and I can- not mess it

75
H.
up; no no, no no no no no no to move from news to dee - jay. To -

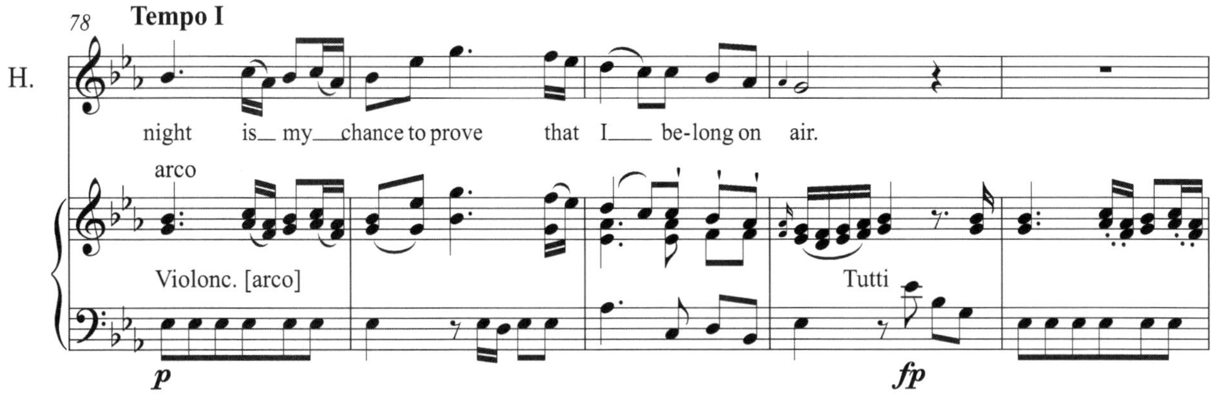
78
Tempo I
H.
night is my chance to prove that I be-long on air.
arco
Violonc. [arco]
Tutti
p
fp

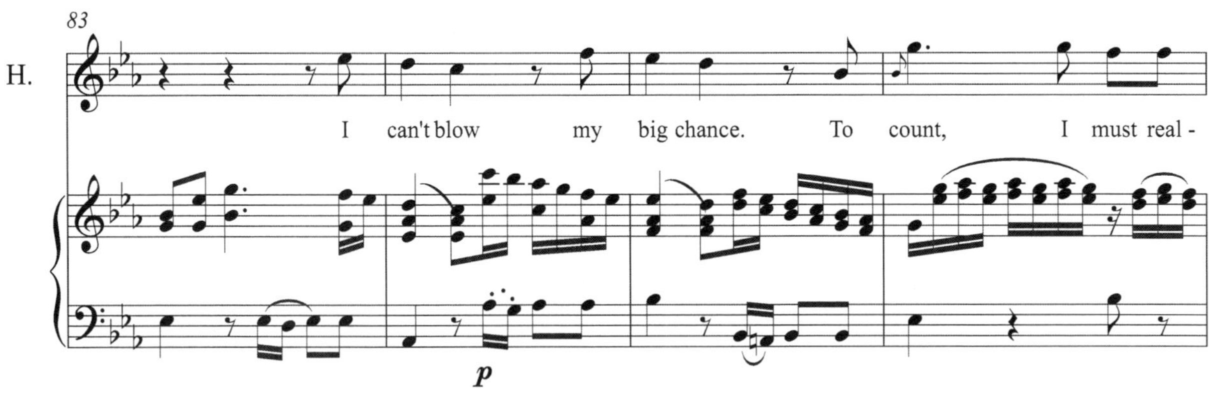
83
H.
I can't blow my big chance. To count, I must real -
p

87
H.
ly shine, and show that I have star qua - li -

92
H.
ty. To prove I be - long on air!
p

96
H.
To - night is my big chance to prove that I be-long on

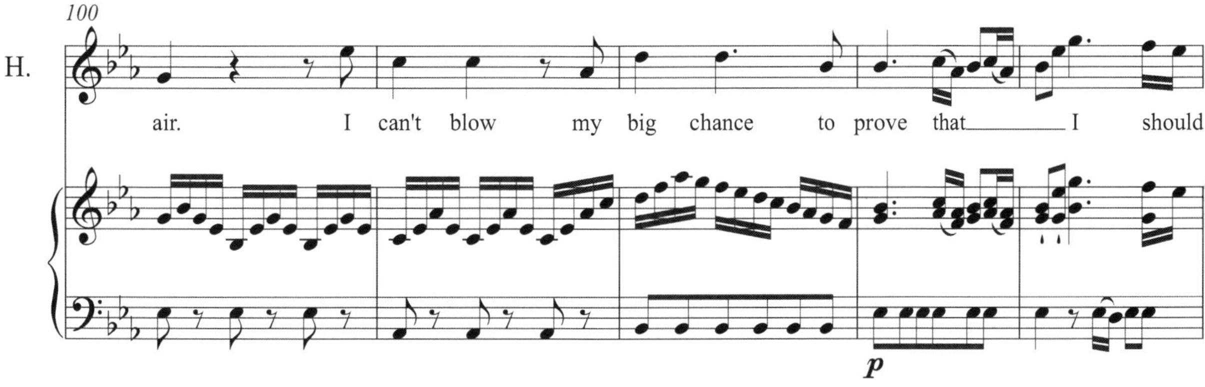
100
H.
air. I can't blow my big chance to prove that I should
p

105
H.
be on the air. I can't blow my
fp
p

110
H.
big chance. To - night I must shine like stars to prove that that

114
H.
I be-long on air
Ah

118
H.
ah
ah
ah
ah
To - night
I
fp

123
H.
must shine like a star to show I be - long,
I must I must I mustshine like a star to show
sf p sf p sf
p
cresc.

127
H.
that I be - long,
I must I must I must I must show that I be - long,
that
fp
sf p sf p sf
p
cresc.
fp

131
H.
I should be on, I should be on air, I
p

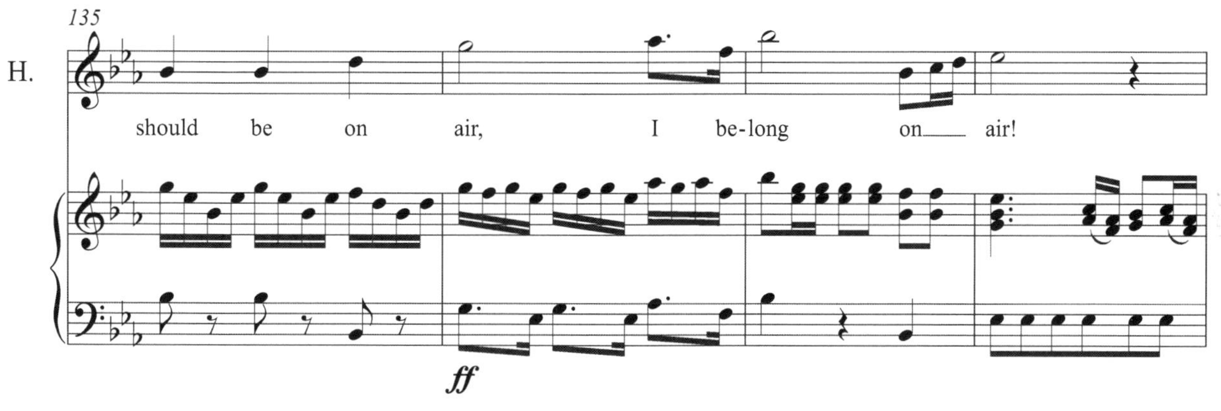
135
H.
should be on air, I be-long on air!
ff

139
H.

143
H.

3. In A Clearing

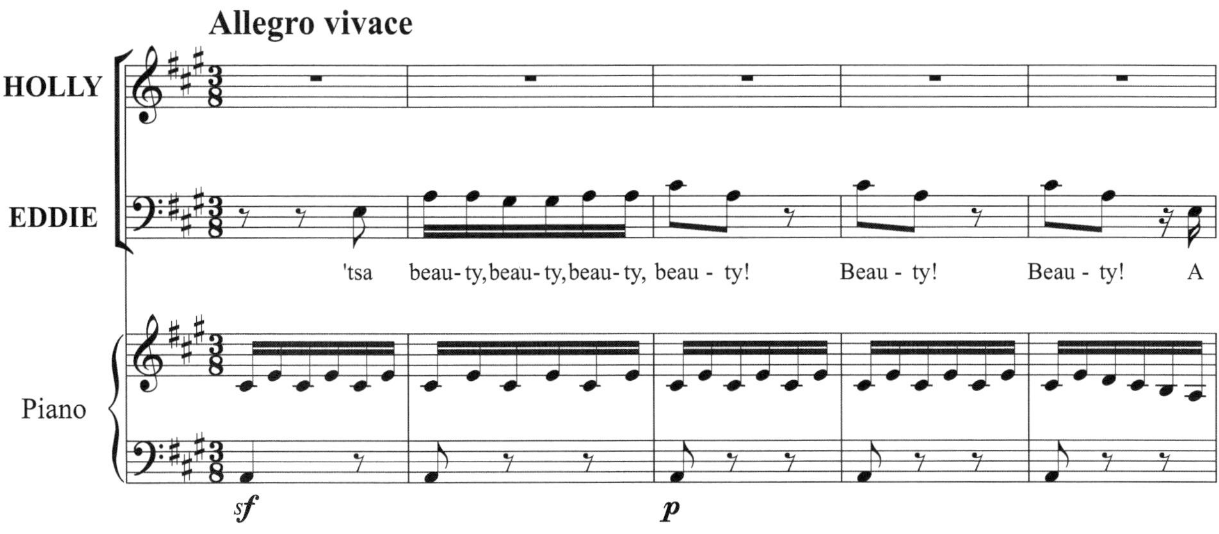

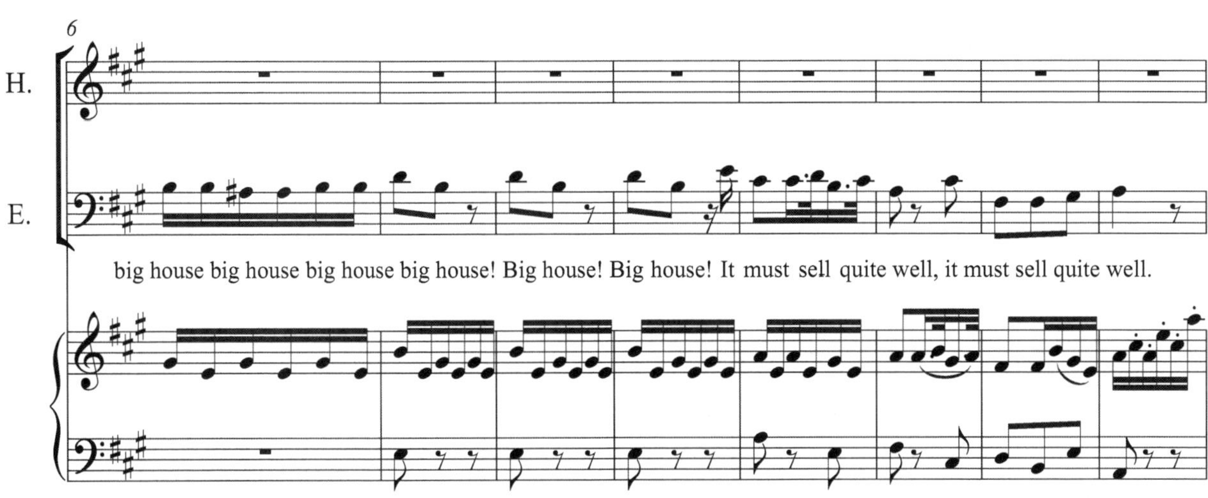

22
H.
E.
tell me now, what is the pro-blem, can I help?
A fart is a fine thing, it
sf
sf

30
H.
E.
makes peo-ple smi-le. A fart is a fine thing, it makes for big laugh-ter. Make it loud and make it bump &
sf
sf p
cresc. poco a poco

38
(Ironic amente)
H.
Ser - ious -
E.
squeak and make it stick y! Like this, like this: qui qui, qui qui.
fp

47
H.
E.
ly?
I am as se-ri-ous as a heart at-tack so li-sten up and li-sten up tight. You
f
p
fp

56
H.
E.
hear me? "In A Clear ing" "In A Clear - ing" needs a punch i - er
fp

64
H.
E.
Hold your hors - es. I think the sketch plays fine.
line... or end- ing. Sure,
ff

73
H.
E.
(Marvin hammers)
Mar vin!. Your ti-ming is per- fect.
(Lagnuno da se)
it does, but...
Just
Tutti
ff
p
sf
sf

80
H.
E.
This is no time to think.
It's fu-nny e nough, it will get laughs. It is
hear out my think ing, it's not real-ly fu - nny. May-be if we add a mon key it could be a cash cow. Just

88
H.
E.
fu-nny e - nough it will get a good laugh. It is fu-nny e-nough it will get a good laugh!
add a mon key, it could be a cash cow. Just add a mon - key it could be a cash cow!
p
rf
fp sempre
p

96
H.
This fe - llow is cra - zy! Oh no! This night is
(Eddie leaves)
E.
rinf

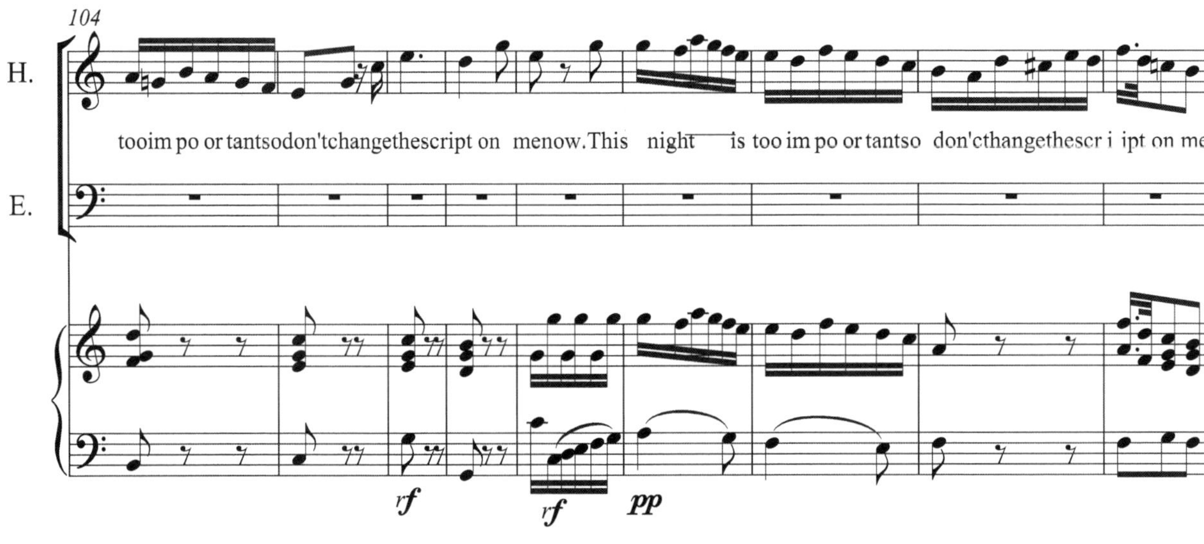
104
H.
tooim po or tantsodon'tchangethescript on menow.This night is too im po or tantso don'tchangethescr i ipt on me
E.
rf
rf
pp

113
H.
now, don'tchange the script right now
(Eddie returns)
E.
fp
ff

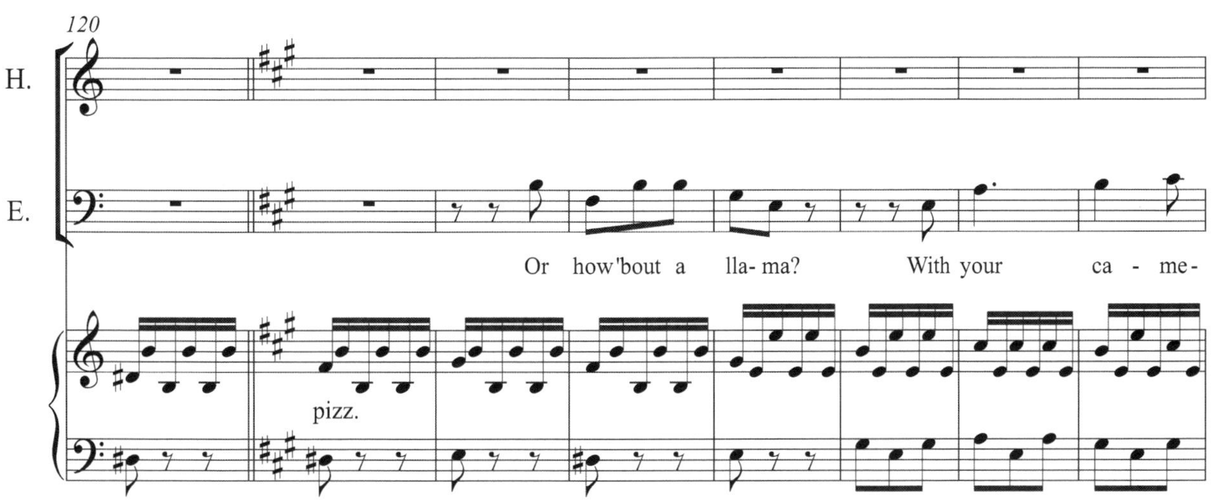
120
H.
E.
Or how'bout a lla- ma? With your ca - me-
pizz.

128
H.
Be hardnow to switchfromthe scriptwhichwe staged... and re-hearsedand whichtakesplace in Ye llow
E.
ra?
arco

136
H.
stone Park. Oh me, oh, me oh, me. It's
E.
Oh, don'tbelike_ this, oh, don'tbeli_ke this, oh, don'tbe_li ke this, it's a piece of cake.
p e leggiero
fp
p

145
A piacere
Allegro
H.
a que-stion of blo-cking, a que-stion of blo-cking, you are freak-ing me out!
E.
Per-haps a hi-ssing
ten.

153
H.
E.
li-zard, per-haps a hi-ssing li-zard! It could pick up the pace, think of what it

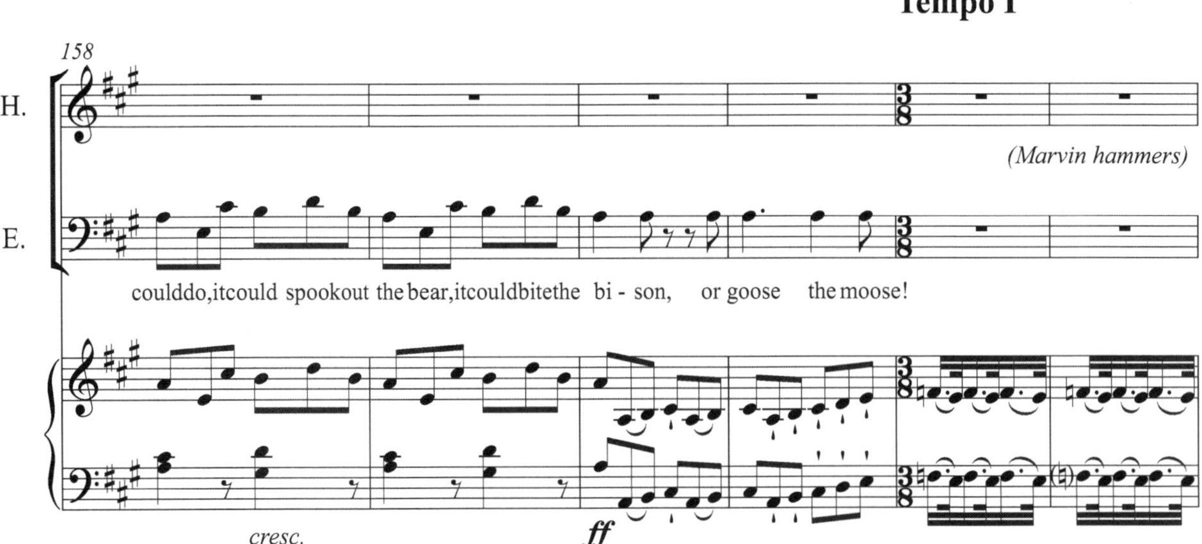
Tempo I
158
H.
(Marvin hammers)
E.
couldo, it could spook out the bear, it could bite the bi-son, or goose the moose!
cresc.
ff

164
(Marvin hammers)
(Marvin hammers)
H.
Mar-vin! Your ti - ming is_ per - fect! Mar vin!
E.
Love it, love it! Love it, love it!
p

171
(Marvin hammers)
H.
Mar - vin! This is no time to___ think. It is fun - ny e - nough
E.
Love it, love it, love it, love it! Just hear out_ my_ think-ing, please hear out_ my_
p

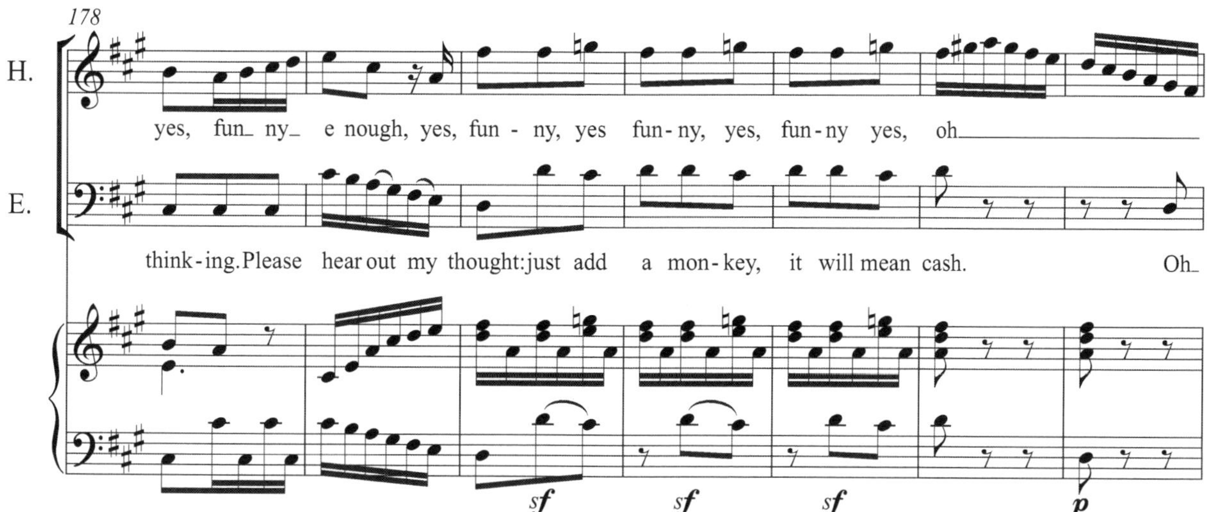
178
H.
yes, fun_ ny_ e nough, yes, fun - ny, yes fun-ny, yes, fun-ny yes, oh
E.
think-ing. Please hear out my thought: just add a mon-key, it will mean cash. Oh_
sf
sf
sf
p

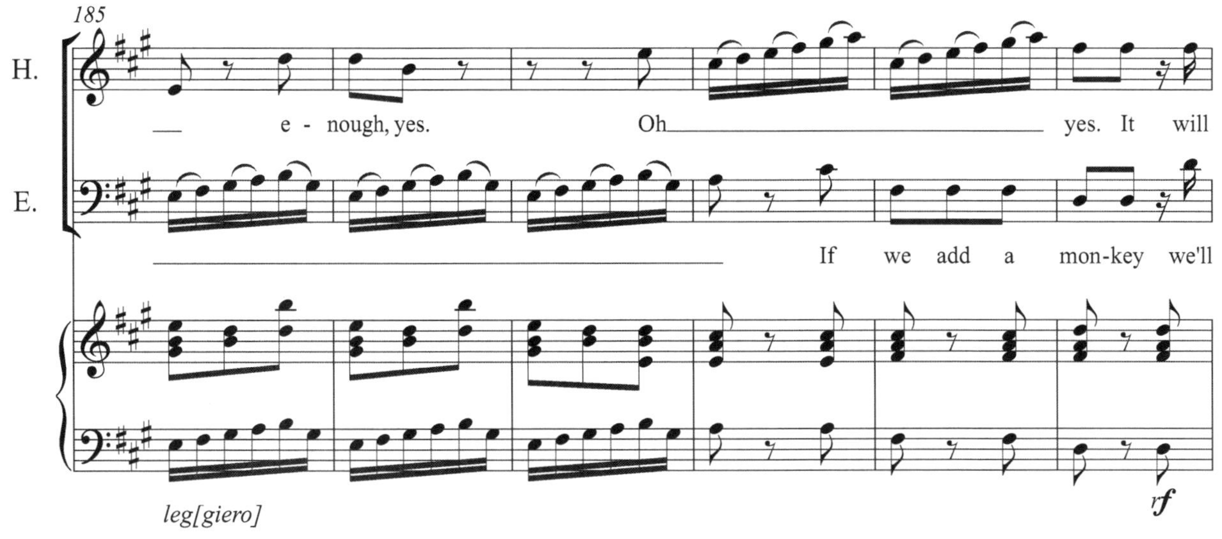
185
H.
E.
e - nough, yes. Oh yes. It will
If we add a monkey we'll
leg[giero]
rf

191
H.
E.
get a good, oh It will get a good, oh
get a cash cow. We'll get a cash cow, we'll

Più stretto

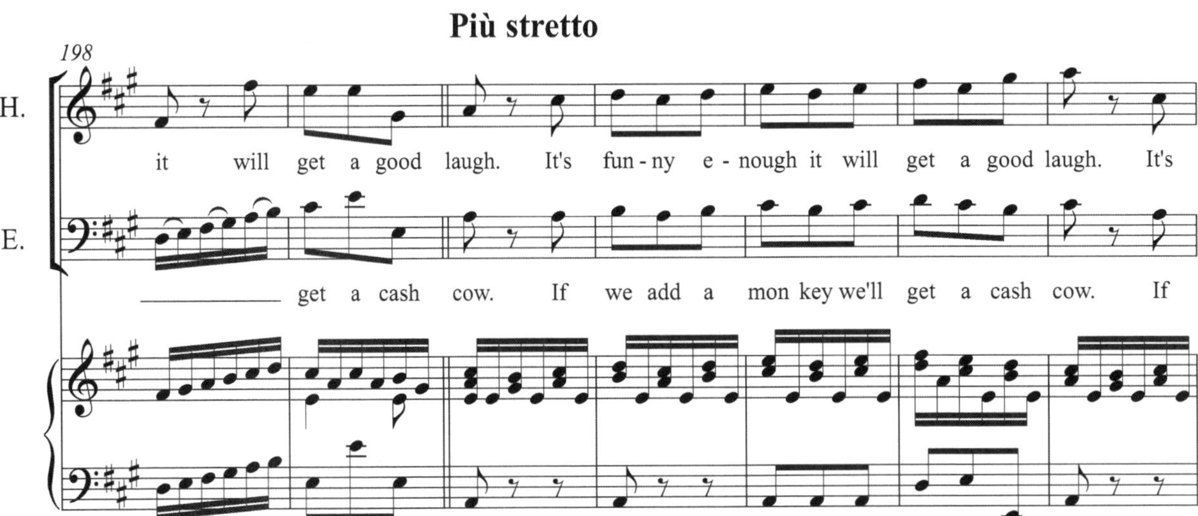
198
H.
E.
it will get a good laugh. It's fun - ny e - nough it will get a good laugh. It's
get a cash cow. If we add a mon key we'll get a cash cow. If

205
H.
fun - ny e - nough it will get a good laugh. It will
E.
we add a mon - key we'll get a cash cow yes sir, get a cow get a cow

211
H.
get some laughs. Ah laughs.
E.
get a cow get a cow get a cow get a cow get a cash cow!

218
H.
E.

4. Cod Piece Dining

10
H.
S.
set list?
Whose big i - dea
E.
p
14
H.
(Points at Eddie)
S.
was this?
You are get-ting way too cock- y.
E.
17
H.
S.
You are get-ting way too cock- y, cock- y. And you know what that means, and you know what that means,
E.
cresc.

20
H.
(Points at Stephan's coffee mug)
S.
don't you?
Su-per lat- te, su-per lat-te. Lots of froth ing, lots of fro-thing. Just a hint of ci-nna
E.
f p f p f p f p
24
H.
S.
mon. Lots of fro- thing, lots of fro- thing! Just a hint of cinn - a mon. -
E.
f
28
H.
Just a thought, just a thought; e-ver heard, e-ver heard of de- caf?
S.
We are
E.
p
f

32
H.
S.
E.
rea - dy! Tell me what sketch you like the best.
A -dren
p
36
H.
S.
E.
A-dren - a - line? Cod Piece
a - line, A-dren - a - line A-dren-a-line Ad - ven - tures?
f
40
H.
Cod Piece Di - ning! Cod Piece Di - ning! Cod Piece Di - ning, Cod Piece
S.
Di - ning!
E.
Cod Piece Di - ning! Cod Piece Di - ning, Cod Piece Di - ning, Cod Piece
p
cresc.
f

43
H.
S.
E.
Di- ning!
We all a - gree, then, that it will be Cod Piece Di-ning Room that clo-sesout the end of the
Di- ning!
sf p
sf p
48
Allargando non molto
first act.
Bea-ver-zill- a!
It's go-nna kill 'em!
Bea-ver-zill- a!
imitando la parte
f
52
It's go-nna kill them!
What a-bout My Break-fast With Boo- boo? My Break-fast With
fp
sf

56
H.
S.
Boo-oo- boo?
Should it stay in the show, e - ven if it is a fun - ny
E.
sf
59
H.
I a-ssure you it be - longs in, taste- less, taste- less, taste- less, taste- less, taste- less taste-less thought
S.
bit?
E.
I a-ssure you it be - longs in, taste- less, taste- less, taste- less, taste- less, taste- less, taste-less thought
p
62
H.
is.
I a - ssure you it be - longs in.
S.
But it real - ly is so rude...
But it real - ly is so
E.
is.
I a - ssure you it be - longs in.
f
p
f

65
H.
I a - ssure you it be - longs in. There is co-me-dy in truth!
S.
crude.
There is co - me - dy in
E.
I a - ssure you it be - longs.
Taste- less, taste- less, taste- less,
p
fp
68
H.
I a - ssure you
S.
truth, yes, there is co - me - dy in truth, yes, there is co - me - dy in truth. You both make ve-ry good
E.
taste- less, taste- less, taste- less, taste- less, taste- less. There is co - me - dy in truth. I a - ssure you it be
fp
fp
71
H.
it be longs in, be- longs, taste- less, taste - less taste - less thought
S.
points here, I be lieve you make good points, taste- less, taste- less, taste- less, taste- less, taste- less, taste-less thought
E.
longs in, I a-ssure you it be- longs, taste- less, taste- less, taste - less, taste- less, taste- less, taste-less thought
punta d'arco

74
H.
S.
E.
is!
It be-longs
in.
is!
It is real-ly gross- ly, gross- ly...
You've con-vinced
is!
Tutti f
p
rinf
78
Yes!
me.
It's no Cod Piece,this is
true.
Yes!
It be-longs
Tutti f
p
rinf
81
rallentando
You've con-vinced
me. Bea-ver-zi- lla!
It's go-nna kill 'em!
Bea-ver-zi- lla!
in.
imitando la parte

85
In tempo
H.
S.
E.
It's go-nna kill 'em!
How 'bout My Break-fast With Boo - boo?
Should it
fp
fp
88
stay,
should it
still
be in the show e-ven though it
is
a fu - nny
fp
fp
f
91
I a-ssure you it be-longs, I a-ssure you it be-longs, I a-ssure you it be-
bit?
I a-ssure you it be-longs, I a-ssure you it be-longs, I a-ssure you it be-
p
f p
f p

94
H.
longs in the show. Taste- less,taste less,taste-less though it is.
S.
Taste less,taste-less,taste- less, taste- less,taste less,taste-less though it is. You've con-vinced me that
E.
longs,taste - less taste- less,taste- less, taste- less,taste less,taste-less though it is.
f p
f
97
H.
There is co - me - dy in truth! There is co - me - dy in
S.
there is co - me - dy in truth! You've con-vinced me that there is co - me - dy in
E.
There is co - me - dy in truth! There is co - me - dy in
f
100
H.
truth! Taste - less though it is, though it is. I a-ssure you
tr
S.
truth. Taste- less, taste- less,taste- less, taste- less,taste- less,taste-less though it is. You a-ssure me it be -
E.
truth! Taste- less, taste- less,taste- less, taste- less,taste- less,taste-less though it is. I a-ssureyou it be -
Celli p
Tutti f

103
H.
S.
E.
tr
__ taste - less though it is. 'me - dy in truth! Sure, it be -
longs in, taste - less, taste - less though it is. There is co - me - dy in truth! There is co - me - dy in,
longs in, taste - less, taste - less though it is. 'me - dy in truth! Sure, it be -
106
H.
S.
E.
longs in. There is co - me - dy in truth!
co - me - dy in truth!
longs in. There is co - me - dy in truth!
ff
109
H.
S.
E.

5. Jello

Allegro moderato
HOLLY
STEPHAN
EDDIE
DEBBY
Piano
HOLLY
No - Jell - o?
and you call this a
fp
fp
5
STEPHAN
co - me- dy?
I'd like to
but
we'd lose our
de - po- sit.
fp
fp
9
EDDIE
Oh, great, we're let - ting ra - tio-nal con-si - der-a - tions rule.
Ra-
cresc.
f
12
tion - al - i - ty will kill our show.
p

6. Different Things

31
a - part.
So granted,
I don't know them all
34
that well.
And they seem
to want dif - fer - ent things.
They seem
37
to want
diff'rent things
They
seem to want diff' rent
sf
40
things.
Ah
grant-ed,
I don't know
them well,
but I think
f
p
f

43
they_ want_ diff' - rent_ things.
p
f
p
46
Ed-die will be tor- men - ted
f
p
49
as he pur- sues
act - ing.
Ed - die will, will be tor -
52
men - ted I see, poor boy, I see that he will be tor-men - ted.
f
ff

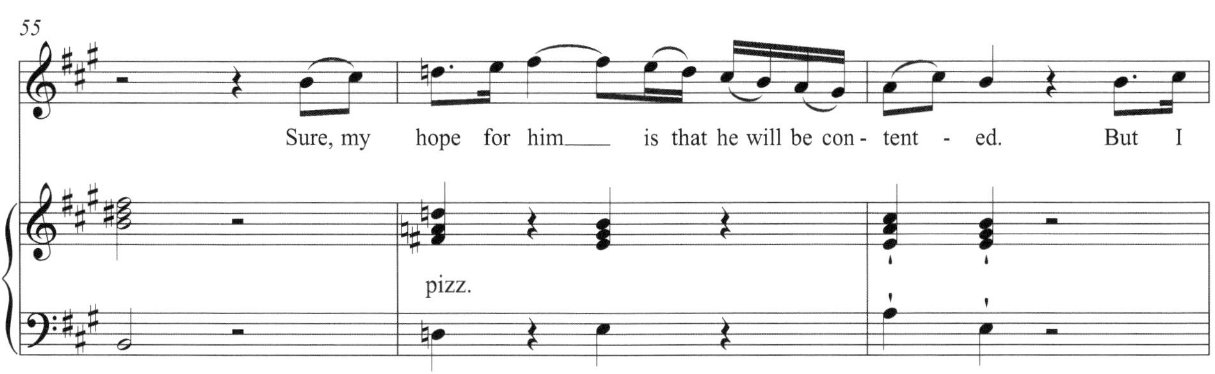
55
Sure, my hope for him is that he will be con - tent - ed. But I
pizz.

58
fear in- stead that he will be tor-men - ted. I hope he'll be con

61
tent - ed but I fear for him, I do. Ah ah

64
ah ah ah ah ah ah

67
ah. Act-ing is a tough ra-cket.
Act-ing is a tough ra-cket and I fear, I fear for
[arco]
p
poco f
71
him, oh
oh, I sure fear for him.
Yes, act
74
ing,
such a rack - et.
Poor Ed - die, I see he'll be tor
77
men - ted as he pur-sues his craft.
Oh,
sf

79
ah
ah ah ah ah ah ah
tr
p
f
83
ah. He'll be tor-ment-ed pur-sue-ing his craft. He will be pur_ su - ing_ his craft, so I
sf
sf
87
fear for him, I fear for him, I fear for him, I fear for
91
him.
ff
95
dim.

7. Geo

Allegro
DEBBY
DAVE
(Dave enters, flipping through a large Geo car catalog)
STEPHAN
Piano
p
fp
fp
p
4
DEB.
DA.
ST.
fp
fp
8
DEB.
DA.
Why are you so pen - sive? Why
ST.

12
DEB.
DA.
are you so torn up? Gon-na
ST.
fp
fp
15
DEB.
DA.
buy my old grand - dad a Ge - o. Gon-na
ST.
fp
fp
19
DEB.
DA.
buy my old grand - dad a Ge - o. It's a
ST.

22
DEB.
DA.
great time to be here in show - biz! A great time to be in show biz -
ST.
sf
fp
sf
25
DEB.
DA.
ness! It's a great time to be show - offs, it's a
ST.
p
28
DEB.
DA.
great time to be big show- offs! It is such a great time to be here in show biz -
ST.

31
DEB.
DA.
ness, I'm ha-ving such a great time be-ing in show-biz!
ST.
f
34
DEB.
DA.
ST.
p
f
p
37
DEB.
I am so - rry, I'm on - ly pro-jec - ting these stray
DA.
ST.

40
DEB.
DA.
ST.
thoughts I now find are de-press - ing.
If you say it hurts when you go
43
like that, then I say you should not go like that.
Hey! This
46
Have you
song, it should be just a-bout me!
tr
f
p

52
DEB.
DA.
ST.
thought, oh, a- bout, hmm, which mo - del?
There are ma ny sty-les for_you to
57
choose from...
No, don't pick that, don't pick that, not the Met- ro, it will ne-ver fit your key - boards.
So be
61
So now I
ware, you would not get much use.
sf

64
DEB.
DA.
see your point.
Your point?
Make a point.
Make a
ST.
I've got one!
f
p
68
DEB.
DA.
point if you want me to li - sten.
Tell me.
ST.
Oy vey!
72
DEB.
DA.
Tell me your point and I'll li - sten.
Just a
ST.
p

75
DEB.
DA.
car, don't you know, that will thrill me. Just a car fast e-nough for some
ST.
sf
sf
78
DEB.
Just a mi - nute. I'm con fused, for grand - dad, that will
DA.
fun, not too fast, though. That will thrill me. For grand - dad
ST.
Just a mi - nute. I'm con fused, for grand - dad, that will
p
81
DEB.
thrill, not too fast, fast e - nough? Say, have you gi - ven some thought to the
DA.
not too fast, fast e - nough.
ST.
thrill, not too fast, but fast e - nough?
rinf

84
DEB.
DA.
ST.
Priz - m?
It is real - ly a Toy-
I just want to find a car that I can give grand - dad.
You con - fuse me. Who's the
87
o - ta, a Co-rol - la, I know, what a shock!
That will thrill me when I take him out for a ride
car for? I don't know what you mean "for grand dad."
91
The Storm is spor - - ti - - - er!
thrill when I take him out for a ride
I don't know what you mean when you say "for grand - dad."

94
DEB.
DA.
ST.
The Storm is spor - ti - er!
Car that will thrill me when I
I don't know what you mean when you say "for grand dad."
sf
p
98
DEB.
DA.
ST.
Take a test drive, try the Storm and the
take him for a ride. Can't you tell me which car will
Oh, to go for a ride. Try the
101
DEB.
DA.
ST.
Priz - m. Why not try the Priz - m? Why
thrill me? I just want a,
Track - er for four wheel drive,
sf

104
DEB.
not try the Priz - m? You might like it. You might
DA.
I just want a car that thrills me when I
ST.
for four wheel drive. Just a
sf
p
107
DEB.
like it.
DA.
drive it. Tell me the car, tell me the car, if you do not I will hold my
ST.
mo- ment,I am think-ing of a car.
110
DEB.
I am think- ing, I am think- ing,I am think- ing, I am think- ing,I am think- ing,
DA.
breath
ST.
I am think- ing, I am think- ing,I am think- ing, I am think- ing I am think- ing
p
cresc.

113
DEB.
got it! You might like the
DA.
— O - kay, tell me what it is. If you
ST.
wait! If not four-wheel
Tutti
f
115
DEB.
Storm. You might like the
DA.
please. I might like the
ST.
drive, you might just like the
p
117
DEB.
Storm. You might like the Storm.
DA.
Storm. I might like the Storm.
ST.
Storm. You might just like the Storm.
f

120
DEB.
DA.
Thrill me!
Thrill me!
ST.

8. Suppose

Andante espressivo come nell' Overtura
DEBBY
Piano
p
Largo
4
DEB.
Sup-pose, sup-pose they make it? How would
sf
7
DEB.
that change our lives from now? What would it mean to our lives, to our_ life to-
sf
9
DEB.
ge - ther?

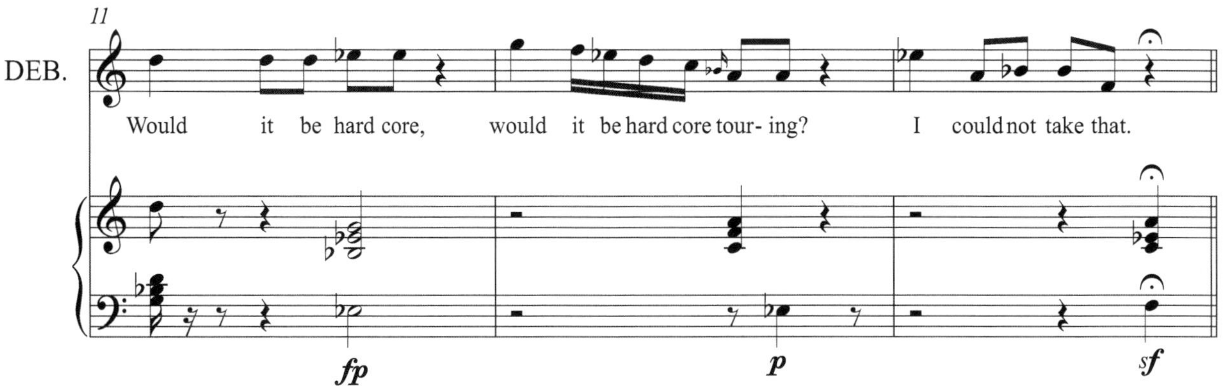
11
DEB.
Would it be hard core, would it be hard core tour- ing? I could not take that.
fp
p
sf

Larghetto
DEBBY
Piano
p
5
DEB.
tr
tr
8
DEB.
11
DEB.
rinf

13
DEB.
p

9. Butterflies

16
H.
Poor me, my sto-mach's roi-ster-ing. Oh, on a night so ma-gi-cal, to fail would be too
p
mf
pp
21
H.
tra-gi-cal. But - ter-flies now sur - round me. I can't
3
3
mf
p
25
H.
blow my chance to shine. Poor me! So why de
28
H.
stroy me? Poor me! De- stroy me.

30
H.
Poor me! De stroy me. It seems like I am lo - sing my nerve at the worst,
p
34
H.
the worst pos - si - ble worst time.
rinf
sf
37
Andantino
H.
I think that to go on now I might need to see a
42
H.
doc - tor. But, if this fee ling will pass, I think I can blow their

47
Allegro
H.
socks off!
If I can just get past me!
To show what I can
51
do.
If I can just get past me I will
f
p
54
show what I can do!
f
p
58
What a great night! It's not hard to, to pre -

62
H.
tend that_ I___ will do well.
When I
66
H.
go on I would pre-fer not to up - chuck.
Keep my
70
H.
eyes firm-ly, firm-ly on the prize.
I will make do and I will go on. I did
fp
fp
fp
74
H.
not come here just to curl up and die!
If I can just get past me.

78
H.
If I can just get past, if I can just get past me, if I can just get
rinf
81
H.
past. Un-stop - a-ble, won't stop!
f
p
85
H.
I will go on now. I will show them all how it should be done.
89
H.
I will cap-ti - vate, I will cap-ti-vate them with my en-er - gy. They will see my
f

93
H.
ta - lent and they will all re-ward me.
I will
97
H.
make do, make do, make do, I'll go on now.
I will
101
H.
make do, make do, make do, I'll go on.
I will go on and im - press them, for
p
105
H.
sure, and show them how, and show them how it should be done, yes,
f

109
H.
show them, yes, show them, I will have to show how it should be
p
cresc
112
H.
done, how it should be done, how
a poco
a poco
f
115
H.
it should be done I will show them how it should be done!
p
119
H.
sf
p

124
H.
128
H.
f
132
H.
135
H.

10. Torn Down

DEBBY
STEPHAN
Piano
Torn down?
That is their in-ten- tion.
Torn down?
ff

4
DEB.
ST.
Torn down?
It seems no e- vi-dence of our ex- ist-ence can escape their wreck ing ball.
p
f

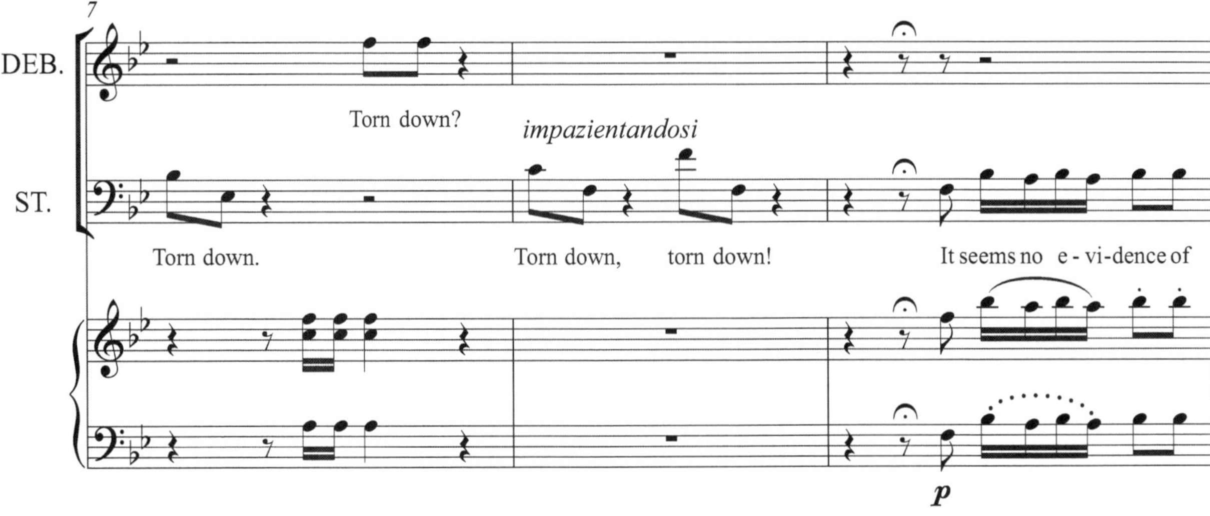
7
DEB.
ST.
Torn down?
impazientandosi
Torn down.
Torn down, torn down!
It seems no e - vi-dence of
p

10
DEB.
ST.
our ex - ist - ence can es-cape their wreck-ing ball. Got no sense of his - to -
rinf
f

12
DEB.
It's not fair. How can they do this? Like they don't care a - bout
ST.
ry.

14
DEB.
their shows?
sotto voce
ST.
And ap-pa - rent - ly they're go-verned by a high - er rate of re-turn meet-ing
dol.

17
DEB.
ST.
This, the best place to see
rooms; ca-ter-ing mark-ups; audi'o-vis-ual rent- als...

20
DEB.
ST.
Loose Ties!
Or to see Shel-ley and Kel- ly? To see Shel-ley and Kel- ly? So co
p

23
DEB.
ST.
My thought ex-act- ly.
zy.
Here, yes I'd hoped to do
f
p

26
DEB.
That's the end of the song!
ST.
great things.
I'd like to've seen Su-san
p

29
DEB.
Ah and Beth Mc In- tosh!
ST.
Carl- man.
Can't be-lieve they'd tear this down, can't be-lieve they'd tear this
f

32
DEB.
ST.
down.
Here I've seen some great acts, ma - ny times, ma - ny times. So much
sciolte
rinf

35
DEB.
ST.
Dead-ly Er- nest,Dead-ly Er- nest.
ta - lent!
It dis-gusts me what they're do - ing; oh, this is nice, oh, this

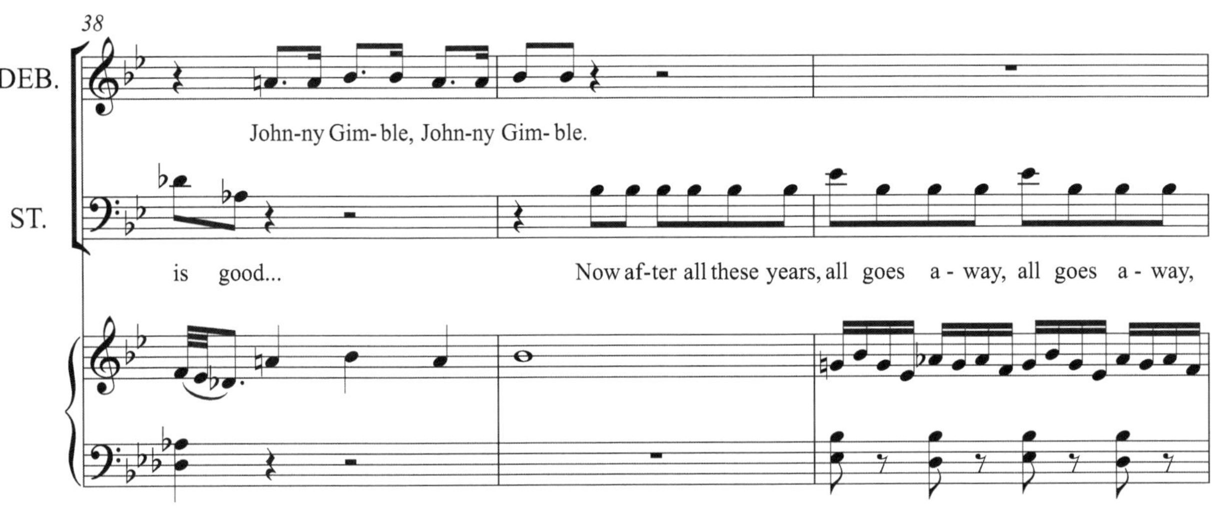
38
DEB.
ST.
John-ny Gim- ble, John-ny Gim- ble.
is good...
Now af-ter all these years, all goes a - way, all goes a - way,

41
DEB.
ST.
(whistles)
like that!
It makes me sick just to think a-bout it, just to think a -

44
DEB.
ST.
What a waste of space, oh, what a waste of space, it sick-ens me, now!
bout it.
sciolte
sf
p
cresc.
sf
sf

47
DEB.
ST.
Side, talk-in' 'bout Side Chan-nel
Well, I think it could have been much worse,

50
DEB.
ST.
Swing Band. Saw Saw-mill Creek here and Doc Wat- son.
it could have hap-pened be-fore our show. De-spite this set-back we
sf

53
DEB.
ST.
must pre - pare the cast now to put on the show. Got to pre-pare to put
f

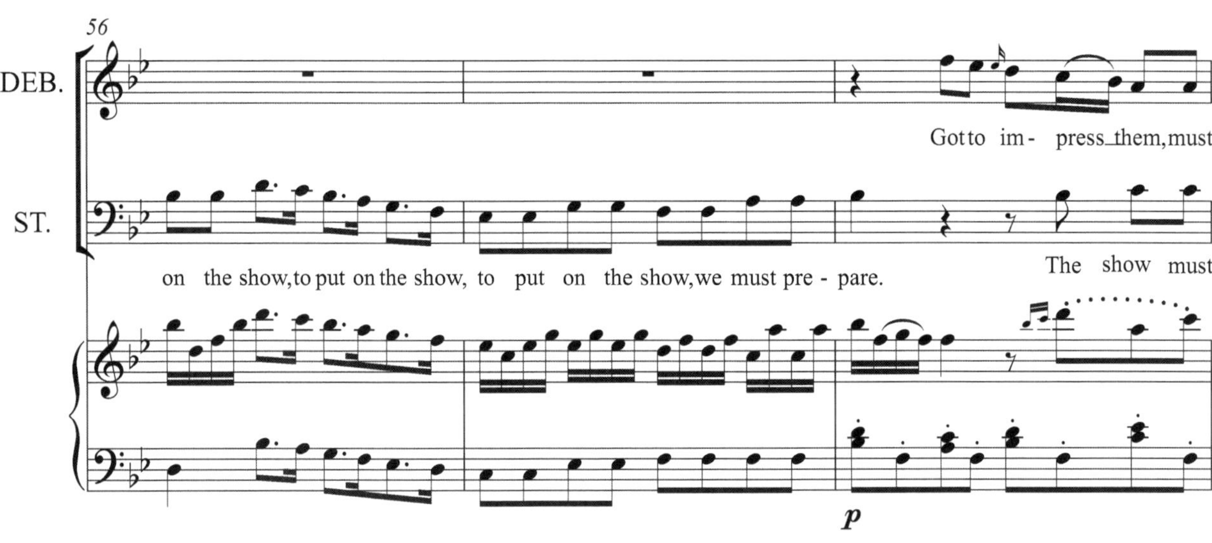
56
DEB.
Got to im- press them, must
ST.
on the show, to put on the show, to put on the show, we must pre - pare. The show must
p

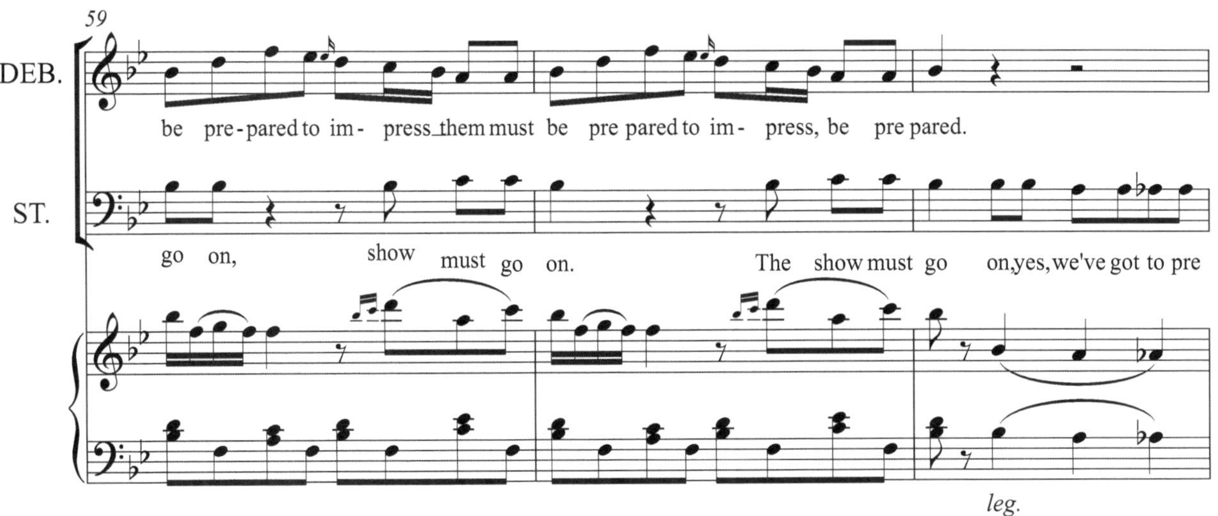
59
DEB.
be pre-pared to im- press them must be pre pared to im- press, be pre pared.
ST.
go on, show must go on. The show must go on, yes, we've got to pre
leg.

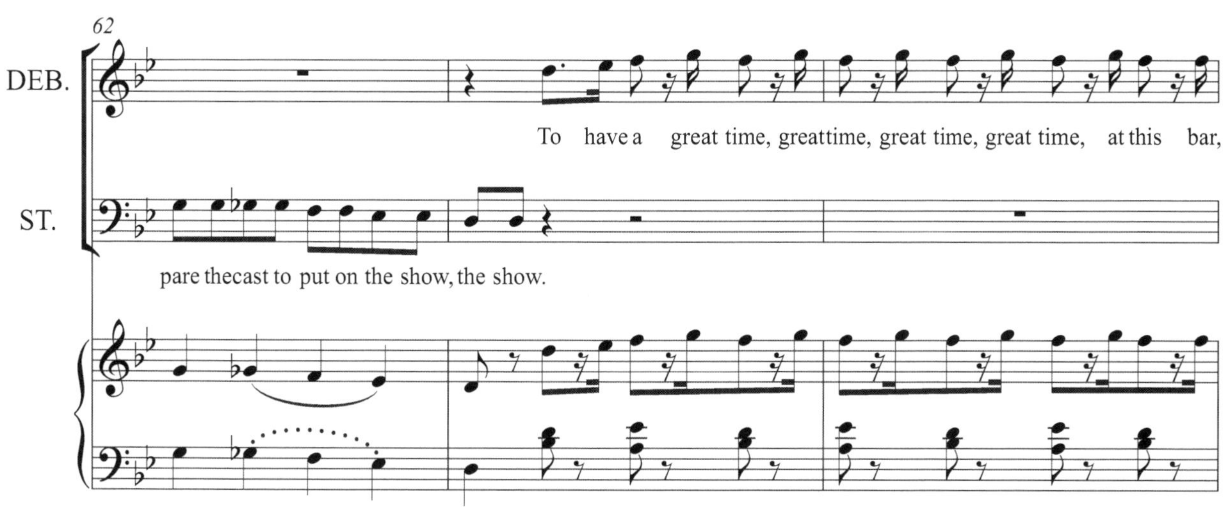
62
DEB.
To have a great time, greattime, great time, great time, at this bar,
ST.
pare thecast to put on the show, the show.

65
DEB.
oh you don't have to be a su - per - star.
ST.
You don't have to be a
sf
p

68
DEB.
You don't have to be a
ST.
star, no, you don't have to be a star. You don't have to be a

70
DEB.
star, no, you don't have to be a star, have a great time at this
ST.
star, no, you don't have to be a star, have a great time at this
fp

72
DEB.
bar.
To have a great time, great
ST.
bar. You don't have to, you don't have to, you don't have to be a star.
p

75
DEB.
time, great time, great time at this bar, ah you don't have to be a
ST.
Have a great time at this bar don't be a
sf
p

78
DEB.
star
You don't have to be a
ST.
star. To have a great time. To have a great time you don't have to be a
p

81
DEB.
star
You don't have to be a
ST.
star. To have a great time. To have a great time you don't have to be a
p

più Allegro
84
DEB.
star. Be a star to be a star, no, to have a
ST.
star. You don't have to be a star, no, you don't have to be a star, no, you don't have to be a
p

87
DEB.
great time at this bar, you don't have to be a star to have a
ST.
star to have a great. You don't have to be a star to have a great time at this
f

90
DEB.
great time. To have a great time at this bar, you don't have to, you don't have to be a
ST.
bar, no you don't have to be a star, not at this bar, you don't have to be a

93
DEB.
star to have a great time at this bar, no, you don't have to be a su-per
ST.
star to have a great time at this bar, no, you don't have to be a su-per
ff

96
DEB.
star.
ST.
star.
100
DEB.
ST.

11. Opening Night

15
ST.
sotto voce
trou - per! You trou - per! If you on - ly will per
p

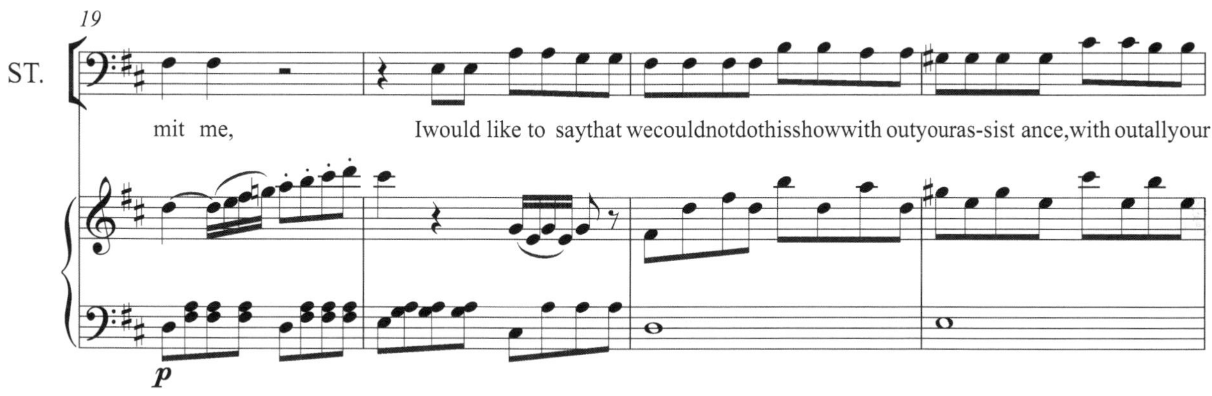
19
ST.
mit me, Iwould like to saythat wecouldnotdothisshowwith outyouras-sist ance,with outallyour
p

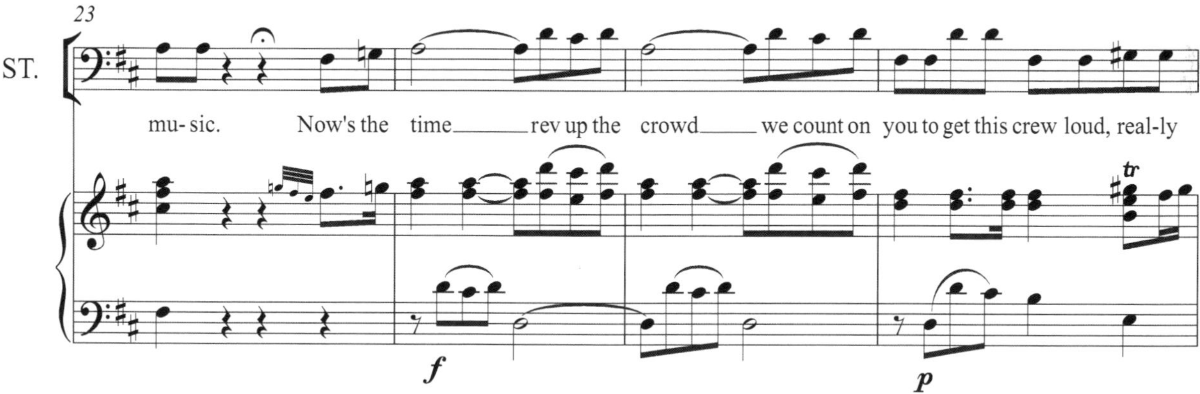
23
ST.
mu- sic. Now's the time rev up the crowd we count on you to get this crew loud, real-ly
tr
f
p

27
ST.
loud, Op' ning night our time has come, and we know our lives will ne-ver be quite the
tr

31
DA.
ST.
Do you real - ly think I have such
same. Yes, we know our lives will ne-ver be the same.
f
p

35
DA.
ST.
ta- lent? You show taste, im-pres-sive as dis
There can be no doubt a-bout it, there can be no doubt a-bout it.

39
DA.
ST.
cern- ing. I must
There can be no doubt a - bout it, there can be no doubt a - bout it.

42
DA.
ST.
say, you are im - press - ive when it comes to your taste a-bout mu

45
DA.
ST.
si - cians.
Yes, I pride my-self on my im-mac - u-late taste, I do, I do.
f
ff

48
DA.
ST.
Check it out, man, the chicks dig
p

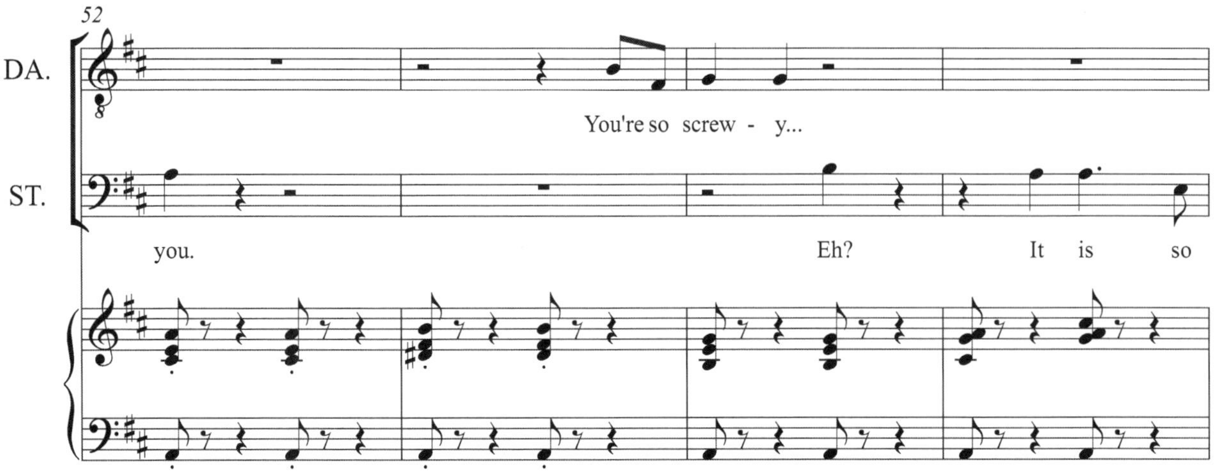
52
DA.
ST.
You're so screw - y...
you.
Eh?
It is so

56
DA.
ST.
ob - vious.
Take it for grant-ed if you wish to.
If you think that you are, you're that
p
p

60
DA.
ST.
kind of guy.
You think that you're that kind of guy,
then you're that kind of
sf
p
f
p

64
ST.
guy.
3
3
3
3

66
DEBBY
DEB.
I've
come to
show
my
sup - port
as you go
on
for the

69
DEB.
first
time.
I'm
sure you'll
knock
'em
all
dead
in the

73
DEB.
ais - les,
and
your
re - pu - ta - tions
will
be
ce-ment
tr
f
p

77
DEB.
ed by the - morn - ing, yes. I real - ly hope you all have - a great time. I real
sf
f
81
DEB.
ly hope that you all have a great time, that you will look back in the morn-ing and be hap - py.
rinf
f
85
DA.
p
My sent - i-ments, my sent-
p all'orrechio
ST.
What a - bout it my friend?
p
88
DA.
i - ments. My sent - i- ments, my sent - i - ments.

Allegro più Moderato
DEBBY
DAVE
STEPHAN
Piano
Am I read-y to go
94
DEB.
DA.
ST.
I've no doubt this is you mo-ment.
Play with
on yet?
What is your most fer-vent de- sire?
97
gen - ious.
Try to make it so I feel it when you spit-take.
Play with

100
DEB.
DA.
ST.
pas- sion!
Make me feel it!
Earn
the ad - mi - ra-tion of your au - di - ence.
p
f
104
I want to hear
your o - pin - ion.
Please stick a-round
past the
She is
so cute!
What a
wo- man!
Got
to
get
to
know her
p
108
Well,
I've got
to run,
now, I'm
due
out
front to
col-lect
tic-
show.
I
want
to
hear
your
o-
now.
She
is
so
cute!
What
a

110
DEB.
kets. Real - ly, I must be go
DA.
pin - ion. Please stick a - round past the show so I can get to know you.
ST.
wo - man! Got to get to know her now, to know her now.
rinf
sf
113
DEB.
ing. Real - ly, I must be go - ing.
DA.
Oh, please stick a-round please stick a-round please stick a-round past the show. Come see
ST.
Get to know her, get to know her got to get to know her now.
f
116
DEB.
I will see what I can do, then.
DA.
me at in - ter - mis - sion. Please don't
ST.
p
f
p

119
DEB.
DA.
cast me as a de - lin - quent, the ve-ry thought makes me
ST.
121
DEB.
Don't be sure of what I'm think- ing, life is real - ly not that simp - le. Please ex
DA.
shud- der.
ST.
cresc.
124
DEB.
cuse me now, I must be go
DA.
ST.
Tutti
f

127
DEB.
DA.
ST.
ing.
I don't know what you see in him.
rinf
p
rinf
130
DEB.
DA.
ST.
I am real - ly so much be - ter, I don't know what you see in this
p
f
133
DEB.
DA.
ST.
He does a mean Jell - o churn - er. He slays
fel - low..
fp

136
DEB.
DA.
ST.
me, he slays me, he slays me with his chur - ning.
sf
rinf
mf
140
I want to hear your o - pin - ion. Please stick
She is so cute! What a wo- man! Got to
144
Well, I've real - ly got to go now. No, I real - ly must be
a-round past the show. I want to hear your o
get to know her now. She is so cute! What a

147
DEB.
gone. Now. Now
DA.
pin - ion your o-pin - ion tell me now. I want to hear what you
ST.
wo - man! Got to get to know her now. She is
rinf
149
DEB.
go. You see
DA.
think now. I want to hear, I want to
ST.
so cute! I've got to know, I've got to
sf
f
151
DEB.
I real - ly have to go now, it's no - thing per - so - nal.
DA.
hear, I want to hear what you think now, what you think now. Yes,
ST.
know, I've got to get to know her now. Must get to
sf

153
DEB.
I've got to go now. Please, un-der-stand it's no-thing per_ so_ nal_ at_
DA.
please stick a-round now. Please stick a - round now past the show I_ want to_
ST.
know her. Must get to know her. Got to got to got to
sf
156
DEB.
all, no, not - per-so - nal, not per - so - nal at all.
DA.
know you, please stick a-round please stick a - round, please stay.
ST.
now. Got to get to know her got to get to know her know her now.
159
161
tr
rinf

12. Finished

Allegro Presto

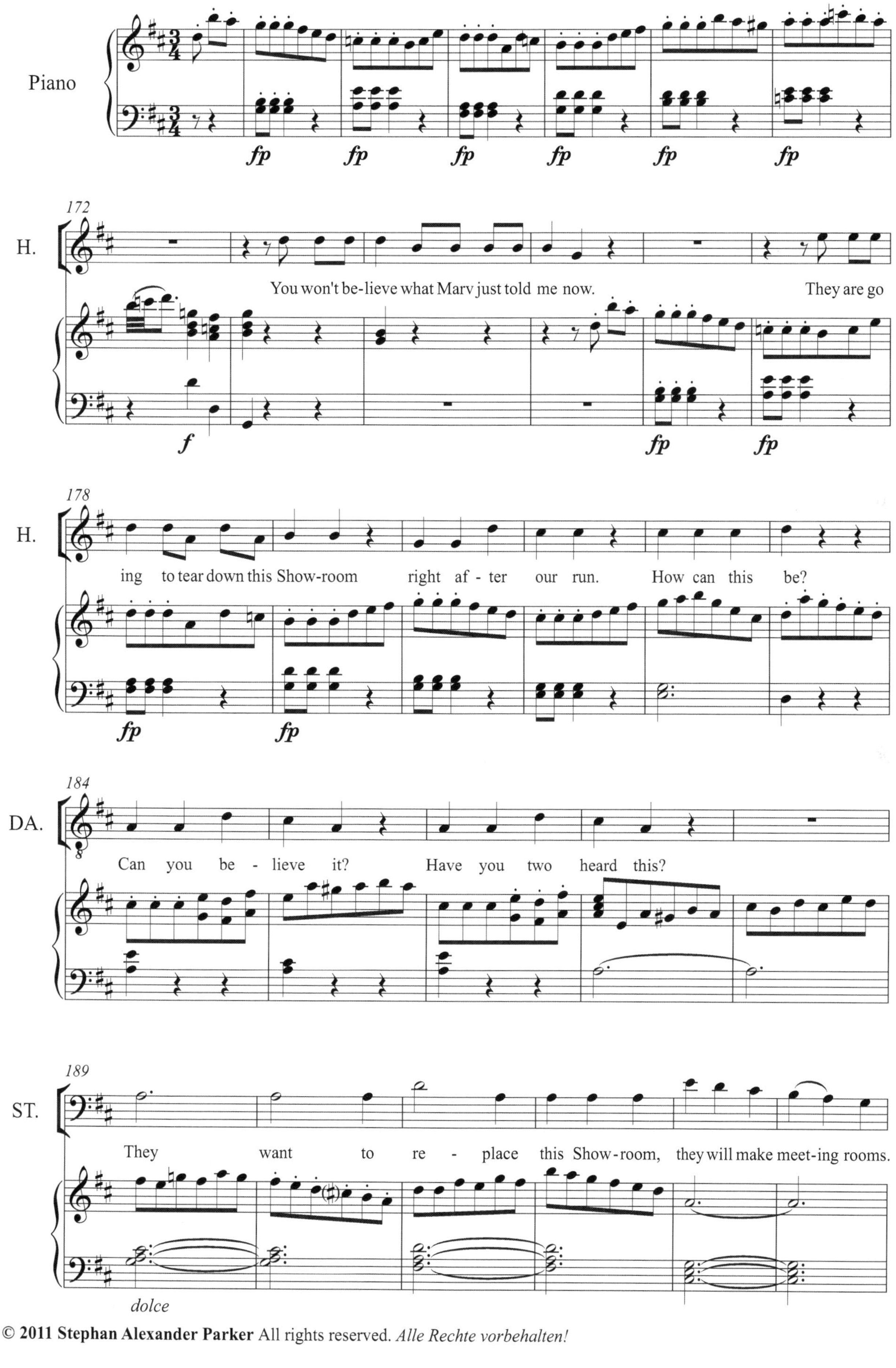

Piano

fp fp fp fp fp fp

172

H.

You won't be-lieve what Marv just told me now. They are go

f fp fp

178

H.

ing to tear down this Show-room right af - ter our run. How can this be?

fp fp

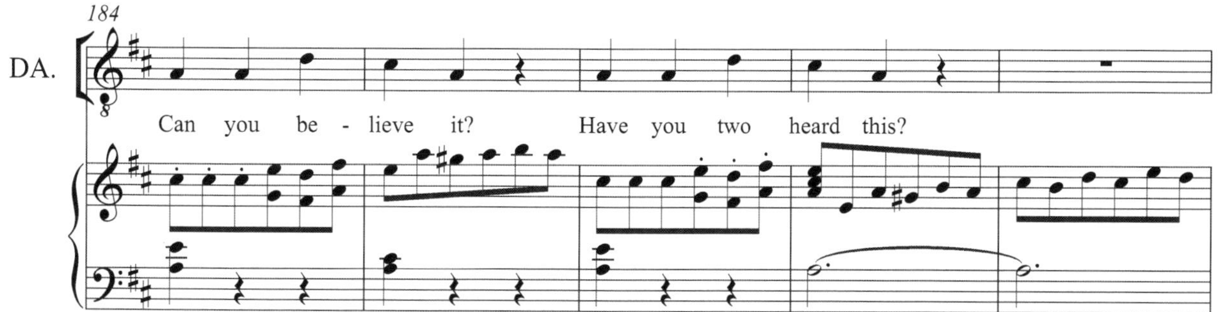

195
ST.
Next thing you know Fred's Mar-ket will be-come So-the-by's.
201
ST.
At least we still have Dir - ty Jack's Wild West, Wild
208
H.
ST.
Say it ain't so, Joe.
West Theat - re.
214
H.
Did you know a - bout this?

220
DEB.
I hadheard some thing.
H.
"Webothhadheard,webothhadheardsome
ST.
Yes, it'strue,weboth hadheard,webothhad heardsomething.
f
p
f

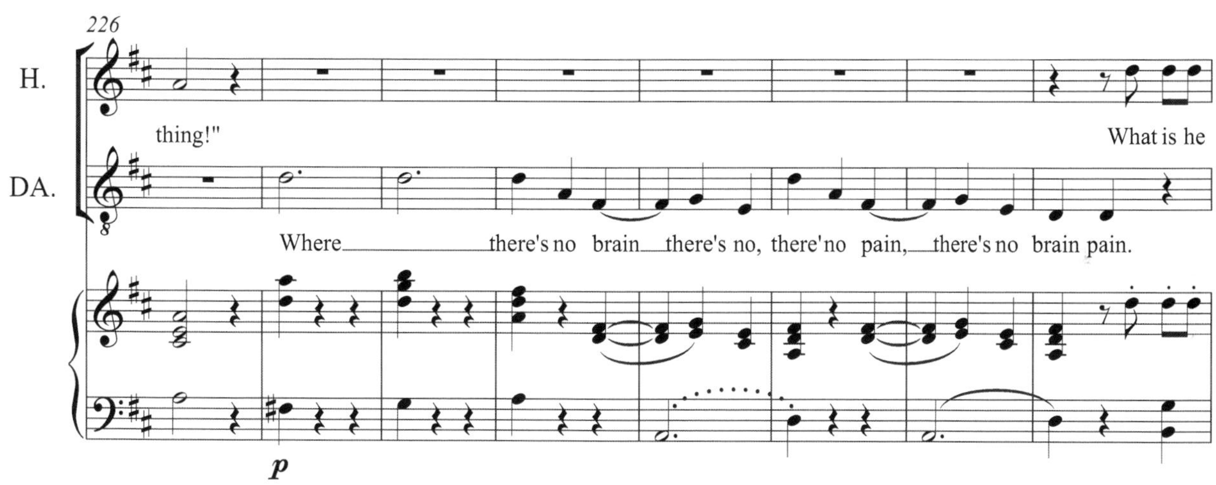
226
H.
thing!"
What is he
DA.
Where there's no brain there's no, there'no pain, there's no brain pain.
p

234
DEB.
I can't be lieve we heard no - thing 'til now.
H.
say- ing,what is he say - ing now?
I can't be
fp
fp
fp
fp

240
H.
lieve this, this isn't right. How can they do this? It's so, so un- fair. How can they do this?
246
DEB.
I can't be-lieve it. I can't be-lieve it, I can't be
H.
How can they do this? How can they do this?
251
DEB.
lieve it. For me oh!
H.
They are such dun - ces!
257
DEB.
the de- vils!
ST.
We've got to fo-cus now, we've got to stop this!

262
DEB.
If they think we are fin - ished,
H.
If they think that we're fin
DA.
They think we're fin - shed.
ST.
We've got to get their at-ten- tion now. They think we're fin - ished.
p
rinf

267
DEB.
they don't know what they just
If theythinkwe'refin ished,wewill showthemwhatfor.
H.
ished, they don't knowwhatthey'veaskedfor, see!
Yes, wewill showthem whatfor.
DA.
They don't know us. See!
ST.
They don't know. See!

272
DEB.
See!
H.
See!
It is so un- fair!
DA.
Oh, boy, are they in for a sur prise...
ST.
Oh, boy, are they in for a sur prise...
How can they
f
p
f

277
DEB.
H.
DA.
ST.
think we're an-y-where close to fin- ished?
Be-cause we're real - ly just get ting
p
f

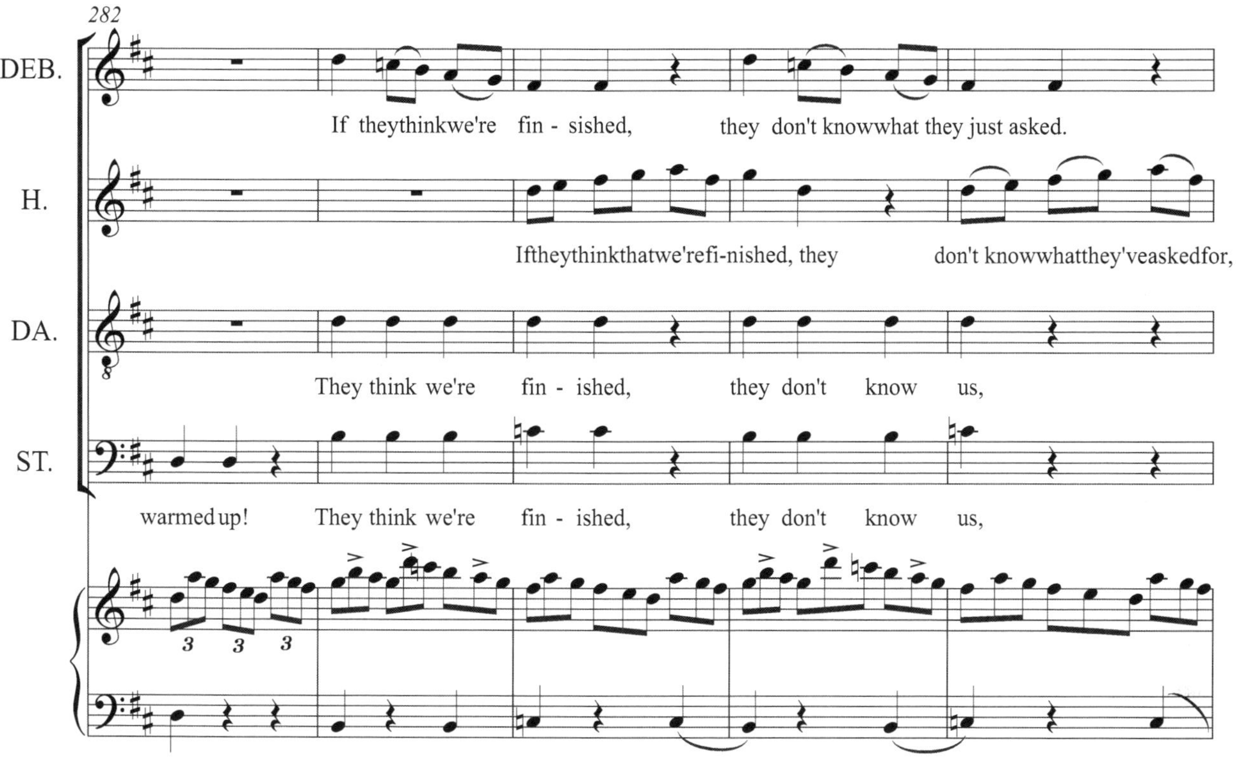
282
DEB.
If they think we're fin - ished, they don't know what they just asked.
H.
If they think that we're fi-nished, they don't know what they've asked for,
DA.
They think we're fin - ished, they don't know us,
ST.
warmed up! They think we're fin - ished, they don't know us,

287
DEB.
If they think we're fin ished, they don't know what they just asked for, see!
H.
see! Yes, they don't know what they just asked for, see!
DA.
see! Oh, boy, are they in for a sur
ST.
see! Oh, boy, are they in for a sur
f

292
DEB.
They think we're fin - ished, we'll show them what - for,
H.
They think we're fin - ished, we'll show them what - for,
DA.
prise! They think we're fin - ished, we'll show them what - for,
ST.
prise! They think we're fin - ished, we'll show them what - for,
3
3
3

297
DEB.
they think we're done, then check this out!
H.
they think we're fin - ished, let them check this out!
DA.
they think we're fin - shed, let them check this out!
ST.
they think w're fin - ished then check this out!
ff

302
H.
ST.
E.
Please par-don me,I justhearda-boutthis. Ihaveaway topro -test,hereI suggest:Let'sen-ter a float, OldWestDaysPa
p
sf
308
H.
ST.
E.
rade, let's en-ter a float, Old West Days Pa- rade!
The Gov-er - nor,
he will be
sf
sf
f
314
H.
This is pre-poster ous!
ST.
This is im possib le!
E.
here!
That'swhatthey tell me.
Take a num- ber.We'dbe so a-nnoy-ing and em-bar
p
f
p
sf

320
H.
ST.
E.
ass - ing in front of, in front of the Guv!
We could an - noy in front of the
sf
sf
f
326
They think we're pat sies, pat sies, pat sies?!
We can pro - test it!
They think we're pat sies, pat sies, pat sies?!
We can pro - test it!
Gov' nor!
We can pro - test it, we can pro - test it
We can an
332
We can an - noy them!
We can an - noy them!
noy them!
We can just push it all as far as it can go here...
cresc.
ff

13. Glory

337
Sostenuto
(to the cast)
DAVE
To - night, my friends, our sto-ry's, we go to
Piano
tr
tr
fp
f

340
(to the audience)
DA.
glo - ry... To serve you is our plea - sure. To serve you is our
p

342
DA.
plea- sure. We pro-mise we will bring this whole place to life once more... You'll
f
p
f

344
DA.
think that to serve you... to serve you is our plea - sure.
p

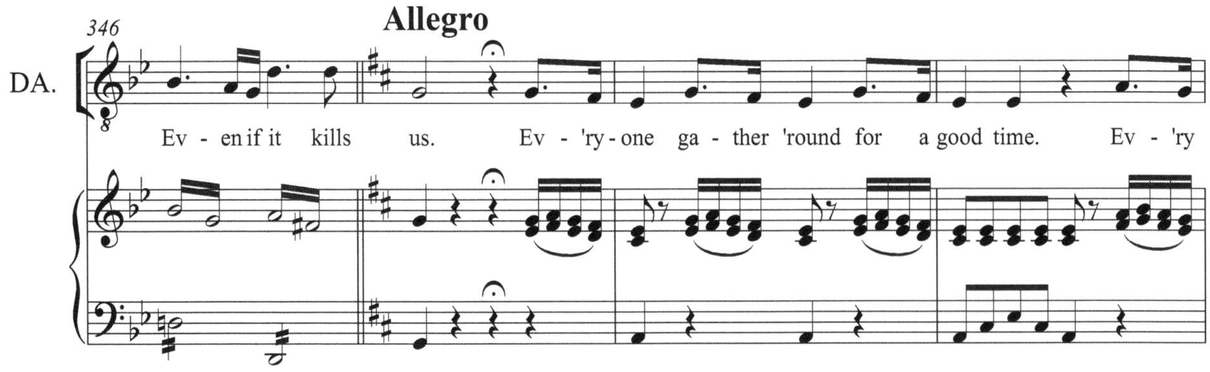
346
Allegro
DA.
Ev - en if it kills us. Ev - 'ry - one ga - ther 'round for a good time. Ev - 'ry

for

350
DA.
one ga - ther 'round for a good time! Laugh at our ex-pense as we're a pri - vate

353
DA.
biz'ness. That does-n't mean we're not a not-for - pro - fit!
f
p

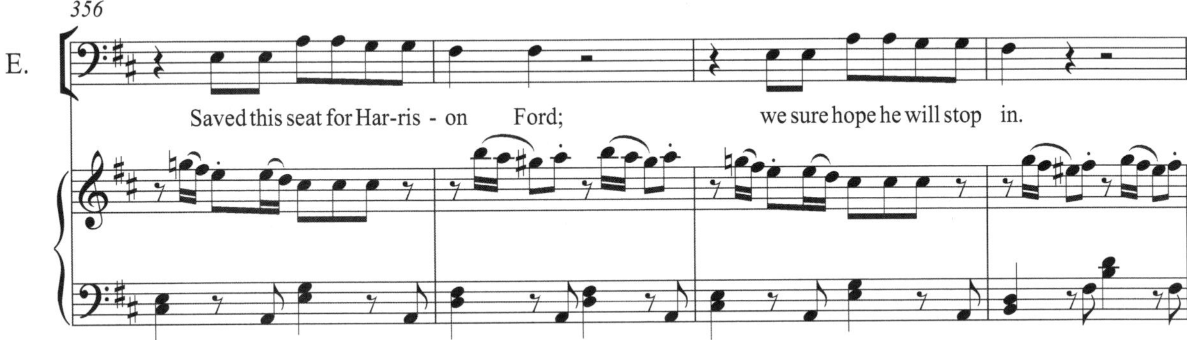
356
E.
Saved this seat for Har-ris - on Ford; we sure hope he will stop in.

360
H.
Watch the an - i-mals as they all come punch in and plan their
363
DEB.
See the boat-men drink their break - fast. It's dis-gust-ing that's for
H.
day.
367
DEB.
sure.
E.
Come stand for the U. S. Na - sal A - ca - de - my ver - sion
369
E.
of, of the U. S. nat - 'nal an - them of the U. S. nat - 'nal

371
H.
DA.
E.
sotto voce
Watch the an - i - mals all
Ev' - ry - bo - dy have a good time!
song!
See the seat for Har - ris - son Ford!

374
DEB.
H.
E.
See the boat-men drink their break- fast!
punch in!
We're dis-gust-ing that's for sure! So won't you come and watch us

377
DEB.
H.
E.
It's fun for the whole fa
It's fun for the whole fa
all as we play rat min ton, play rat minton, play rat min ton or squash?!

381
DEB.
mi - ly! It's fun for the whole fa
H.
mi - ly! It's fun for the whole fa
DA.
Ev' - ry - one can play it!
S.
Ev' - ry - one can play it!
E.

385
DEB.
mi - ly! Road - kill!
H.
mi - ly! Road - kill!
DA.
Ev' - ry - bo dy can play it, yes, we can all play it at one time! Road - kill!
S.
Ev' - ry - bo dy can play it, yes, we can all play it at one time! Road - kill!
E.
Ev' - ry - bo dy can play it, yes, we can all play it at one time! Road - kill!
pp

389
DEB.
H.
DA.
S.
E.
Stand - up! There is one way to, yes, there is one
Stand - up! There is one way to, yes, there is one
Stand - up! There is one way to, yes, there is one
Stand - up! There is one way to, yes, there is one
Stand - up! There is one way to, yes, there is one
f

Un poco più Allegro
392
DEB.
H.
DA.
S.
E.
way to as- sure, yes, there is one way to as-sure a stand- ing, yes a stand-ing a stand-ing o-va - tion:
way to as- sure, yes, there is one way to as-sure a stand- ing, yes a stand-ing a stand-ing o-va - tion:
way to as- sure, yes, there is one way to as-sure a stand- ing, yes a stand-ing a stand-ing o-va - tion:
way to as- sure, yes, there is one way to as-sure a stand - ing, yes a ing a stand-ing o-va - tion:
way to as- sure, yes, there is one way to as-sure a stand - ing, yes a ing a stand-ing o-va - tion:
ff

396
DEB.
Please rise as he plays, he'll now per- form, na tion-al an - them by har-mon-i-
H.
Please rise, he'll per - form na-tion-al an - them. Rise as
DA.
Please rise as he plays, he'll now per- form, na-tion-al an - them by har-mon-i-
S.
Please rise as he plays, he'll now per- form na-tion-al an - them by har-mon-i-
E.
Please rise, I'll per - form the an - them. Rise as
3

400
DEB.
ca played through his nose, na-tion-al an- them. Play har moni-ca on to
H.
he per - forms na-tion-al an- them. Play har moni-ca on to
DA.
ca played through his nose, na-tion-al an- them. To glo -
S.
ca, played through his nose, na-tion-al an- them. Play har-moni - ca on to glo - ry.
E.
I per - form the an- them. Play har-moni - ca on to glo - ry.
pizz.
3

404
DEB.
glo - ry. Play har - moni - ca through his nose. Play har-moni - ca
H.
glo - ry. Play har - moni - ca through his nose. Play har
DA.
- ry through his nose, his nose. Play har-
S.
Play har - moni - ca through his nose. Play har-moni - ca
E.
Play har - moni - ca through my nose. Play har-moni -ca
arco
sf

407
DEB.
on to glo - ry play har-moni ca. Yes, he
H.
moni-ca on to glo - ry. Yes, yes, he will play the an-them through his nose. Yes, he
DA.
moni-ca on to glo - ry. Yes, he
S.
on to glo - ry. Play har-moni ca. Yes, he
E.
on to glo - ry. Play har-moni ca. Yes, I
sf
sf
f

411
DEB.
will play the an - them by nose, by nose.
H.
will play the an - the by nose, by nose.
DA.
will play the an - them by nose, by nose.
S.
will play the an - them by nose, by nose.
E.
will play the an - them by nose, by nose.
ff
Soli
p
414
DEB.
Rise as he
H.
Rise as he
DA.
S.
E.
Tutti
f

417
DEB.
plays, as he plays nation-al an - them.
H.
plays, as he plays nation-al an - them.
DA.
By har-mon - i - ca through
S.
By har-mon - i - ca through his nose.
E.
By har-mon - i - ca through

420
DEB.
Rise as he plays, as he plays as he plays.
H.
Rise as he plays, as he plays, as he plays.
DA.
his nose.
S.
By har-mon - i - ca by
E.
my nose.

423
DEB.
Play harmon-i-ca through his
H.
Play harmon-i-ca through his
DA.
By har-mon-i-ca-by nose. On to glo-ry. Play har-mon-
S.
nose. On to glo-ry. Play har-mon-i-ca
E.
By har-mon-i-ca by nose. On to glo-ry. Play har-mon-

426
DEB.
nose harmon-i-ca through his nos-trils.
H.
nose harmon-i-ca through his nos-trils.
DA.
i-ca on to glo-ry through his nose.
S.
on to glo-ry through his nos-trils.
E.
i-ca on to glo-ry through my nose.

429
DEB.
Road-kill! Stand-up! Glo - ry! There's one way to as-
H.
Road-kill! Stand-up! Glo - ry! There's one way to as -
DA.
Road-kill! Stand up! Glo - ry! There's one way to as-
S.
Road-kill! Stand-up! Glo - ry! There's one way to as -
E.
Road-kill! Stand-up! Glo - ry! There's one way to as -
ff

433
DEB.
sure we get the crowd to get up on its feet right now. He will
H.
sure on its feet. He will get the
DA.
sure we get thecrowd to get up on its feet right now. He will
S.
sure we get the crowd to get up on its feet right now. Get the
E.
sure we get the crowd to get up on its feet right now. Get the
f p fp

437
DEB.
p
get the crowd up on its feet right now. On to glo-ry on to glo-ry.
H.
crowd up on its feet. Play har moni-ca through his nose, yes, on to
DA.
get the crowd up on its feet right now. On to glo-ry on to glo-ry.
S.
crowd up on its feet. Nation-al an-them by har moni-ca through his
E.
crowd up on its feet. Nation-al an-them by har moni-ca through my
fp
fp

a piacere colla parte in tempo
441
DEB.
Play har-mon-i - ca through Yes, he will now play, through his nose, nation-al
H.
glo - ry. Through his nose! Yes, he will now play, through his nose, nation-al
DA.
Through his nose. Nose!
S.
nose, yes, through his nose!
E.
nose, yes, through my nose!
f
p

446
DEB.
an-them. He will now play, through his nose, nation al
H.
an them. He will now play, through his nose, nation al
DA.
He will play har mon-i - ca, yes;
S.
He will play har mo-ni - ca, yes;
E.
I will play har mon-i - ca, yes;

450
DEB.
song. He will play har - mo - ni - ca. Ah Ah
H.
song. He will play har - mo - ni - ca. Ah Ah
DA.
He will play har - mo - ni - ca!
S.
he will play har-mo-ni - ca on to glo-ry through his
E.
I will play har-mon-i - ca! On to glo-ry through my

454
DEB.
Ah
Ah
H.
Ah
Ah
DA.
Through his nose, yes!
S.
nose, yes, on to glo - ry.
List- en, this is what I'm
E.
nose, yes, on to glo - ry.
List- en, this is what I'm
rinf

458
DEB.
There is co - me - dy in truth! Ah
H.
There is co - me - dy in truth! Ah
DA.
There is co - em - dy in truth!
S.
say - ing: there is co - me - dy in truth! Psy-cho
E.
say - ing: there is co - me - dy in truth! Psy-cho
f
p

461
DEB.
Ah
Ah
Ah
H.
Ah
Ah
Ah
DA.
S.
Road-kill. On to glo-ry. Through his nose, yes.
E.
Road-kill. On to glo-ry. Through my nose, yes.

464
DEB.
There is co-me-dy in
H.
There is co-me-dy in
DA.
Psy - cho Road - kill. There is co-me-dy in
S.
List-en, this is what I'm say-ing: there is co-me-dy in
E.
List-en, this is what I'm say-ing: there is co-em-dy in
rinf
f

Più stretto
468
DEB.
truth!
Ah
H.
truth!
Ah
DA.
truth!
There is co - me - dy in truth, yes,
S.
truth! There is co - me - dy in truth, yes,
there is co - me - dy in
E.
truth!
There is co - me - dy in truth, yes,
p

471
DEB.
Ah
H.
Ah
DA.
there is co - me - dy in truth!
There is co - me - dy in
S.
truth!
There is co - me - dy in truth, yes,
E.
there is co - me - dy in truth!
There is co - me - dy in

474
DEB.
Psy - - cho
H.
Psy - - cho
DA.
truth, yes, there is co-me-dy in Psy cho
S.
there is co-me-dy in truth! There is
E.
truth, yes, there is co-me-dy in There is real
f

477
DEB.
Road kill, Psy - cho Road - kill,
H.
Road kill, Psy - cho Road - kill,
DA.
Road - kill, Psy - cho Road - kill,
S.
co - me - dy in truth! There is co - me-dy in
E.
co - me - dy in truth! There is co - me-dy in

480
DEB.
Psy - cho Road - kill, Psy - cho Road - kill, Psy - cho Road - kill rules!
H.
Psy - cho Road - kill, Psy - cho Road - kill, Psy - cho Road - kill rules!
DA.
Psy - cho Road - kill, Psy - cho Road - kill, Psy - cho Road - kill rules!
S.
Psy - cho Road - kill, Psy - cho Road - kill, Psy - cho Road - kill rules!
E.
Psy - cho Road - kill, Psy - cho Road - kill, Psy - cho Road - kill rules!

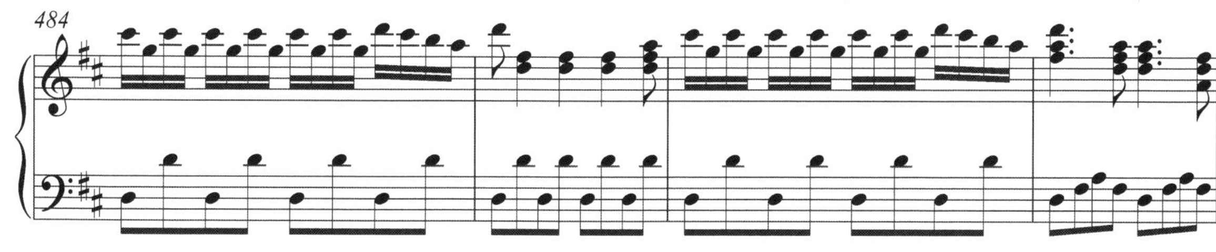
484

488

ABOUT THE AUTHOR

Stephan Alexander Parker began his professional writing career when he noticed that Magic Industries, Inc., publisher of The Magic Magazine, had relocated their business offices to Nashville; he talked his way into a job filling mail orders and ended up writing catalogue descriptions. Within two years, he was shifting inventory between stores and making deliveries for Mills Bookstores. He had plenty of opportunities to gather material directly and through stories he heard while working as a bus driver, whitewater rafting guide, front desk clerk, technical writer, research manager, and light and sound man. After stints in Nashville, Branson, Chicago, Orlando, Jackson Hole, New Jersey, and Washington DC, he now lives in the old railroad town of Gaithersburg, Maryland, with photographer DJ Choupin. He is currently working on *The Annotated Roadkill Opera.* Or his show business memoir, *I Rode With Ben Johnson.* No, probably the opera thing.

Proof

18523270R00076

Made in the USA
Charleston, SC
08 April 2013